Integrating Services
for Troubled Families

❖❖❖❖❖❖❖❖❖❖❖❖❖❖❖❖❖❖❖❖❖❖❖❖❖❖❖❖❖❖❖❖❖❖❖❖

Dilemmas of Program Design
and Implementation

Harold H. Weissman

◆◆◆◆◆◆◆◆◆◆◆◆◆◆◆◆◆◆◆◆◆◆◆◆◆◆◆◆◆◆◆◆◆◆◆◆

Integrating Services
for Troubled Families

 Jossey-Bass Publishers
San Francisco • Washington • London • 1978

INTEGRATING SERVICES FOR TROUBLED FAMILIES
Dilemmas of Program Design and Implementation
by Harold H. Weissman

Copyright © 1978 by: Jossey-Bass, Inc., Publishers
433 California Street
San Francisco, California 94104
&
Jossey-Bass Limited
28 Banner Street
London EC1Y 8QE

Library of Congress Catalogue Card Number LC 78-62563

International Standard Book Number ISBN 0-87589-385-6

Manufactured in the United States of America

JACKET DESIGN BY WILLI BAUM

FIRST EDITION

Code 7825

*The Jossey-Bass Social and
Behavioral Science Series*

Preface

◆◆

"July and August 1970 brought another in the almost endless parade of children's shelter crises in our city. This latest crisis did not arrive unannounced. The city and the state had been made fully aware of the steady deterioration of child care services by innumerable reports and recommendations, from both official and unofficial sources. But again the response was the same overcrowding, crisis, outcry, census brought down through emergency placement programs, overcrowding, crisis, outcry—the acquisition of still another deteriorating building to relieve overcrowding, with this new facility becoming overcrowded almost on the day it is opened. Inevitably, when the glare of publicity and public outrage dims, an uneasy calm settles until the next time" (Citizens' Committee for Children, 1971, p. 1).

So begins a report on the past twenty-five years of child

welfare crisis in New York City. *Integrating Services for Troubled Families* is a history of one project spawned by this concern over insufficient and ineffective child welfare services. The Lower East Side Family Union (LESFU) was established with the stated purpose of preventing undesirable placement of children away from their families.

This history of LESFU differs in several significant ways from the usual program report or evaluation. It is a natural history, describing the program from its inception by a few people through its planning, initiation, implementation, and institutionalization phases. What problems emerged and how they were dealt with in each of the phases is a central concern.

LESFU historians were present through most of the planning phase and continuously through the other phases of the project. They acted as participant observers in organizational activities: board meetings, staff training sessions, worker-client interviews, and interorganizational contract negotiations.

This book provides a model for those interested in integrating service programs; they may replicate or alter it to fit the particular situations in their communities. The focus here is not only on the way services were delivered and the results achieved but also on such concerns as staffing, facilities, fund raising, staff training, interorganizational relationships, and all other variables that affect a program's outcome. Such an analysis should enable child welfare specialists in particular, as well as specialists in such fields as mental health, to replicate and improve on the LESFU experience in their own communities.

There is an additional and equally important purpose of this book. Social programs in and of themselves are not novelties in our country. If anything, the 1960s saw an exponential development of such programs, from prenatal care to geriatric counseling. Similarly, a host of factors have been put forward for the various successes and failures of these programs—inadequate financing, insufficiently trained staff, lack of community support, and so on.

Yet there have been few systematic attempts in the evaluation of these programs to elicit the general principles and practices of program design and policy implementation. The concentration has been on the results achieved or on suggestions for improving specific programs, such as the necessity for community support or the desirability of stable financing.

Hargrove (1975) says a new form of research is needed, one that goes beyond budget, policy formulation, and program evaluation and focuses on implementation estimates—the varying degrees of ease or difficulty involved in implementing program and procedural alternatives. He argues that greater knowledge of how institutions actually work in implementation processes could improve the design of initial program strategies and enhance the successful administrative operation of programs. Pressman and Wildavsky (1973) show how exaggerated rhetoric and failure to estimate implementation problems can scuttle social programs with the broadest political and financial support.

A secondary goal of this study is to add to the knowledge of implementation, the kinds of knowledge required for predicting the consequences of service delivery in one way as opposed to another. Policy and implementation cannot be separated; before policies are set, the ease or difficulty of implementing alternatives should be considered. Such implementation estimates go beyond the usual program planning or policy analysis because they do not stop with simply asking, for example, whether revenue sharing is a more effective way of funding a certain program than categorical grants. They ask the same question but add "in this type of organizational setting." Since implementation takes place in organizations, the organizational ramifications of any dimension of a program are crucial. It is only through such studies as this one that knowledge of implementation can be developed to guide policy analysts and program designers. At present, our ability to make implementation estimates is considerably limited. No one case study can serve as the source of universally applicable ideas and propositions related to program implementation. Nevertheless, greater knowledge and directions for future research should be an important by-product of this study.

To achieve this end as well as to explain how LESFU attempted to prevent unnecessary placement of children, the book is divided into four main sections: planning and policy formulation, program initiation, program implementation, and a final discussion of problems of program design. In each of these sections, the experi-

ence of LESFU will be analyzed in terms of the ideas and concepts
on which the agency based its actions.

Social historians are merely the reporters of what others have
done. Without the help and committed support of the staff and
board, this project could not have been conceived let alone concluded. What follows represents not only the best judgments of the
social historians but the best judgments of those intimately involved
in the daily operation of the program. As the senior historian, I assume full responsibility for any errors of fact or deduction in the text.

The social history was originally designed to provide ongoing
feedback of problems and issues of concern to LESFU's administrators. As will be noted, the difficulties workers had in operationalizing
the service model made feedback from outsiders threatening and
disruptive. The tracking system later developed by LESFU put
control over feedback in the hands of the workers.

Ultimately, regular meetings with top staff members clarified
general issues related to the development of the service model, but
initially the historians had to be extremely careful about not imply-
ing any criticism of individuals or the project. It is no doubt easier
to be the observer than the observed. Observers should give something back to those they observe in addition to the promise of a
future book. Friendliness, support, and emergency assistance are all
necessary aspects of the historian's job.

The social historians followed approximately ten cases from
intake through monitoring. All training sessions and a variety of
different types of convenings were attended. Most public meetings
with provider agencies and team meetings were observed. Case
records were regularly reviewed and interviews were held with almost all LESFU staff members, selected staff members in provider
agencies, and certain board members.

Several people deserve special mention. Bertram Beck, who
is called Henry Rue in the text, was instrumental in conceiving of a
social history and supporting it throughout the project. Thanks are
also due to the Foundation for Child Development, which provided
funds for the social history, and to Trude Lash, called Judith Ash in
the book, who was research consultant to the foundation. Elizabeth
Howe and Marie Weil served as participant observers and were
invaluable assistants. Special thanks are due to my colleague Sheila

Kamerman for rescuing my central thesis from the obscurity of an earlier draft. The LESFU management team, who in the text are given the pseudonyms of Brahms, Windward, Goya, Field, and Taste, spent long and sometimes tiring hours explaining the intricacies of the program to the historians. I hope this study conveys a sense of their diligence and commitment. And last of all, I thank the clients and staff who gave their time to discuss their experiences in the LESFU experiment. What follows demonstrates that this time was not wasted.

New York City   HAROLD H. WEISSMAN
July 1978

Contents

◆◆

Preface   ix

The Author   xvii

1. A Historical Perspective on the Delivery of Services   1

2. Planning a New Model for Integrating Services
    and Preventing Family Break-Up   12

3. Setting Policy: Fund Raising, Community
    Participation, and Client Selection   23

4. Defining Staff Responsibilities and Priorities   37

5. Engaging Troubled Families and Contracting
   for Services   55

6. Using Organizational Tension to Improve
   Service to Families   80

7. Successes and Failures in Integrating Services
   and Helping Families   95

8. Issues, Problems, and Principles of Designing
   Social Programs   121

   References   139

   Index   143

The Author

∙◆◆∙

HAROLD H. WEISSMAN is currently professor of social welfare at the Hunter College School of Social Work, City University of New York. He earned his bachelor's degree in social science from Yeshiva University (1952), his master's of social work degree from the University of Pittsburgh (1954), and doctor of social welfare degree from Columbia University (1966).

Weissman is active in the National Association of Social Workers. He has produced educational television shows and served as consultant to the CBS television series "East Side, West Side," about a social worker in New York City. From 1965–1970 he was assistant executive director of Mobilization for Youth, a pioneering antipoverty agency.

The author of many articles in such professional journals as *Administration for Social Work*, Weissman is also the author of

Overcoming Mismanagement in the Human Service Professions (1973) and *Community Councils and Community Control* (1970). He has served as an editor of *Abstracts for Social Workers* and as editor and senior author of a four-volume series describing the antipoverty programs of Mobilization for Youth.

To Judy
for caring

Integrating Services for Troubled Families

Dilemmas of Program Design and Implementation

A Historical
Perspective on the
Delivery of Services

◆◆◆◆◆◆◆◆◆◆◆◆◆◆◆◆◆◆◆◆◆◆◆◆◆◆◆◆◆◆◆◆

Social problems are associated with religious, economic, political, cultural, and psychological factors. In and of themselves, the problems are seldom really solved but are redefined and moved toward resolution as the limitations and potential of problems, conceptions, and solutions are understood, as Rittel and Webber (1977) note.

In the course of helping hundreds of families, the problem of unnecessary placement of children was not finally solved by LESFU, although the view of the problem and what LESFU could do about it were altered. Rather than see this result as a failure, the central thesis of this study is that redefinition of problem and solution is a necessary step for programs to achieve their maximum effectiveness—by clearly defining whom they can help, through what means, and under what conditions—and for the better understanding of all the factors that contribute to a social problem and its solution.

Programs should be maintained, discontinued, or changed,

and new and different programs begun as these factors are clarified. Most programs are not organized to systematically redefine their goals and procedures; they usually solidify, stagnate, or change wildly and unpredictably in response to conflicting demands generated by their participants. How LESFU managed these demands and gained control over itself is central to this study as well as a central issue in the design of social programs.

Perspective on Child Welfare

"While great strides have been made since infanticide was the preferred and prescribed method of dealing with unwanted children, no society as yet has been able to devise a system that did not create as a residue of its defects a situation in which large numbers of children were left without adequate support, financial and psychological. Child welfare services are designed to reinforce, supplement, or substitute the functions that parents have difficulty in performing, and to improve conditions for children and their families by modifying existing social institutions or organizing new ones" (Kadushin, 1974, p. 5).

Indenture was an early form of foster family care in colonial times. Children would be apprenticed for several years and provided with food, clothing, and other necessities while learning a trade or craft. If indenture was not possible, dependent or neglected children might well find themselves in an undifferentiated alms house. Here they would reside with the lame, the mute, the elderly, the mentally ill, and the criminal.

In the latter half of the nineteenth century, considerable humanitarian concern was voiced about the abuses of both indenture and the mixed alms house. Many states mandated the establishment of institutions solely for children. In New York City, Charles Loring Brace founded the Children's Aid Society. This organization primarily relocated homeless children from urban slums to the farms of the West and Midwest, a program of group emigration and placement that resulted in finding foster family care in farm homes for about 100,000 children between 1854 and 1929.

Although there were compelling economic and humanitarian reasons for this program of emigration, it was criticized almost from its inception as the old indenture philosophy of child labor. In

Boston, under the leadership of Charles Burtwell, a new approach was suggested. Money was paid to foster families for the maintenance of children who might otherwise have been placed in institutions and who were too young to be profitably indentured. Massachusetts also pioneered more careful supervision of children indentured by the state (Kadushin, 1974). There was also interest in developing a way for children to be restored ultimately to their natural parents.

Disputes in social welfare over the best way to care for the homeless, the dependent, and the neglected child culminated in the first White House Conference on Children in 1909. A carefully selected foster home was given the official sanction as the best substitute for the natural home. Foster family care was given a clear preference over institutions.

Yet some sixty years later, when the Citizens' Committee for Children (1971) prepared its report, *A Dream Deferred,* the situation for children in need of substitute care outside of the family was not encouraging. Children's institutions were overcrowded. They had become the modern equivalent of the undifferentiated alms house. All types of children were being mixed together—the delinquent, the neglected, the mentally ill, and those simply in need of temporary care for emergencies in otherwise stable families.

Once placed in foster care, very few children were reunited with their parents. There was a shortage of trained personnel to deal with children either in foster care or in institutions and an increasing difficulty in recruiting a sufficiently large number of desirable foster homes. Institutional care and foster care were expensive, and the funds available for such care were inadequate.

The preceding sixty years had spawned crises and temporary solutions. In 1972, the Lower East Side Family Union (LESFU) was established in order to prevent undesirable placement of children away from their families. To understand why the organization was created at this particular time and why it took the form it did, certain aspects of the history of social welfare must be borne in mind.

Perspective on Service Integration

By the early 1970s, the enthusiasm for the social programs of the Johnson administration's Great Society and the zest for advocacy

and institutional change had given way to questions about accountability and effectiveness. The profession of social work was on the
lookout for a new direction. But when a profession is forced to
adapt, it seldom completely discards old practices. It keeps its basic
forms, adding a new wing or two and changing its perspective but
seldom its foundation.

Certainly one of the foundations of the field rests in what
may be called the "good government" movement, which began
around the turn of this century. In social welfare, the growing concern for rationality and effectiveness manifested itself in a new
agency form—charity organization societies. Starting in Buffalo and
then spreading to every large and middle-sized city in the country,
the societies developed to coordinate and integrate multiple charities.

These societies divided cities into districts, attempting to
register in each district the clients who applied for help, in order to
prevent fraud and inefficiency in duplication of services and to husband available resources. Friendly visitors were provided to ensure
that clients got what they needed but no more than was required.
"Uplift, not alms" was the early motto. As Kahn (1976) has
pointed out, the key components of these societies had been shaped
over several centuries of voluntary and private charity by such
European pioneers as Vives, Von Vogt, Count Rumford, and
Chalmers. The American societies were a new beginning and a
repackaging of older ideas of districting and friendly visiting and of
central organization.

If the charity organization societies were the earliest modern
organizational structure in social welfare, the social settlements rank
a close second. Their workers settled and developed services in the
neighborhood. If rationality and efficiency were early concerns in
social welfare, so too were locality and locally based services, which
formed the core of settlement house programs.

The charity organization societies never succeeded in their
coordination aims. Over the years, they became service-giving
agencies. Their names changed to family service agencies. The
number of "do-good" organizations did not decrease; the hoped-for
coordination dissipated in the struggle for organizational autonomy
and survival.

During the 1930s and 1940s, agency consolidation and

coverage continued the districting pattern, but most programs were really outposts of increasingly professionalized and centralized bureaucracies instead of locally shaped services (Kahn, 1976). As resources periodically became scarce, centralization and consolidation, rather than coordination, was the usual prescription. The large public welfare departments that developed during the Depression took on the form of centralized offices with district branches. As these departments grew in size, they had their own problems of coordination. In the 1940s and 1950s they were concerned with the so-called "multiproblem families," those that received a disproportionate amount of resources and staff time, families that were known not only to public welfare, but to health departments, correctional institutions, psychiatric hospitals, schools, and the like. The welfare departments responded with a variety of case-management techniques, smaller caseloads, programs for reaching out to clients, and, in the case of New York City, locating staff from various departments in one place, "a department store of services."

The 1960s saw renewed concern with the effectiveness of services. Yet the focus—localism and coordination—was not new. The neighborhood service center was developed basically as a mechanism to secure and integrate services for clients in a local area. Information, advice, referral, follow-up, escort, case advocacy, and policy advocacy were the concerns of these centers, along with social action and neighborhood planning. In addition, many of the bold new programs of the 1960s had as their main intent a coordinated effort—for example, the Community Mental Health Act and the Model Cities Program—as well as a variety of educational programs (Kelty, 1976). A common structure that developed from many of these programs was the multiservice center, intended to go beyond referral and advocacy by offering a multitude of services in one location.

An evaluation of these centers noted, "The most recent solution intended to correct the problem [of fragmentation] is the multiservice center. The difficulty is that such centers can sometimes be a collection of previously fragmented services newly fragmented under one roof"; as one angry woman said at a meeting, "Now I can find out in fifteen minutes that they can't help me. Before, it took three weeks" (Sahlein, 1973, p. 7).

One final attempt to deal with the problem of fragmentation and gaps in services was made by the Department of Health, Education, and Welfare in the early 1970s. The edict to separate the staffs of public welfare departments into those concerned with providing cash assistance and those concerned with providing personal social services developed in part from the desire to free some staff members from the burden of dealing with budgets and cash assistance and to make them available to clients requesting personal social services.

Unfortunately, this directive was implemented very poorly; the staff was insufficiently trained and clients were often unaware of the availability of certain services. When clients asked for services, they were provided with one worker, and, if they returned two weeks later, they simply got a different worker. Fragmentation and lack of coordination increased.

An enduring concern in social welfare has been the necessity to find coordinative mechanisms to improve the delivery of services, and an accompanying concern has always been the cost of services. As expenditures for social welfare tripled and quadrupled in the 1960s and 1970s, with seeming attendant inefficiency and waste, concern mounted among governmental officials at all levels. One response initiated by Elliot Richardson, then Secretary of Health, Education, and Welfare (HEW), focused on ways of developing more effective service integration. "The total HEW services impact is less than the sum of its program parts for the following reasons: (1) services programs . . . are not correlated with a common set of national goals and services objectives; . . . (2) are not responsive to the multiple needs of the clients they serve; . . . (3) are not orchestrated through centralized comprehensive planning processes at state and local levels; . . . (4) tend to be narrowly prescribed and rigidly regulated; . . . (5) not only fail to complement one another, they typically do not mesh with other federal programs (U.S. Department of Health, Education, and Welfare, 1971b, pp. 2–6)'.

A memorandum by Richardson (U.S. Department of Health, Education, and Welfare, 1971a, p. 1)' states the aims of services integration as "developing an integrated framework within which ongoing programs can be rationalized and enriched . . . Its objectives must include such things as (a) the coordinated delivery of services for the greatest benefit to people; (b) the holistic approach to the individual and the family unit; (c) the provision of a comprehensive range of services locally; and (d) the rational allocation of resources at the local level so as to be responsive to local needs."

Money was provided by HEW to encourage initiatives by states and cities in developing service integration models; this was called "capacity building." The service integration effort developed its own lexicon, which tended to underscore for some its novelty, yet, as Gage (1976) notes, the service integration movement could not be considered new. Actually, it was part of an established effort to reform governmental service-delivery systems. Documented strengths and weaknesses of other reform efforts could have been used advantageously but were not. A Council of State Governments document (1974) notes that at the state level, human services integration is an outgrowth of an earlier attempt in which states began to reorganize their executive departments.

This reorganization movement, which began at the turn of the century, tried to correct the extensive development of state agencies separately accountable to governors, legislatures, and independent boards and commissions by grouping some agencies, reducing the number of departments, and aiming for management by a single administrator. The umbrella organizations of the 1960s in social welfare, often called "Human Resources Administrations," were set up to include such services as mental retardation, public health, mental health, public assistance, social services, child welfare, corrections, employment, rehabilitation, and others. Such combinations did not necessarily mean that services were integrated; an agency may simply have brought together fiscal, planning, personnel, and support services. The rationale for these superagencies was similar to administrative reform in other sectors of public service—reduction of the span of control and better management and accountability.

LESFU develops as it becomes clear that the human resource agencies have not provided more effective services; the costs of services, especially in child welfare, are skyrocketing; the value of various social institutions is questioned; the movement toward deinstitutionalization quickens; and services integration is being pro-

moted at the federal level as a solution to the problems of fragmentation, narrowness, and waste in social programs. The following
numbered paragraphs, taken from an early LESFU planning document, indicate the concerns of this period.

1. *Integration of services by contract.* LESFU enters into
contract initially with the founding settlements, but later with all
appropriate service-providing agencies. The contract ratified by
both the board of the union and the agencies states that, in instances
of families known to the union and the agency, the agency partially
relaxes its autonomy with the staff of the union monitoring service
to ensure that everything possible is done to integrate efforts to prevent undesirable placement.

2. *Mobilizing community consciousness around family well-
being.* Union staff recruit members of the union, who elect a majority of board members. Members are pledged to assist their neighbors
as much as possible to achieve the goals of the union. Membership
provides the union with the leverage to negotiate and enforce contracts with local agencies, including those which founded the union.
Membership also works to bring new resources into the neighborhood to fill service gaps identified through the efforts of the Family
Union.

3. *An ecological approach to social work practice.* The
ecological approach to assisting families forsakes classical clinical
casework intervention and puts the union's social worker in the role
of organizer of diverse agencies and individuals interested in assisting
particular families. The family is fully involved in all aspects of
planning and execution of the plan.

4. *Practical helps to reduce family stress.* The Family Union
tries to reduce pressure on the family that leads to child placement.
Homemakers and housekeepers on union staff are used to provide
immediate relief. When temporary placement is required, the child
can be placed in homes in the neighborhood, identified and licensed
through the efforts of the Family Union.

5. *Empowering families to be effective social advocates for
their children.* In all of the work of the union, there is recognition
that professionals must involve parents in planning, make clear to
them their rights and their children's rights, and train them, where
necessary, in the responsibilities of parenthood. Through enabling

families to become social advocates on behalf of their children's needs, the union becomes a vehicle for influencing social policy.

The services of the project will be provided through three service teams. Each team will include a team leader with a master's degree in social work, five social work associates, three homemakers, three housekeepers, and a clerk-typist. The ethnic composition of the teams will reflect the composition of the area served.

Clearly, LESFU was and is concerned with several major problems in the delivery of social services: development of a technique of integrating services, the viability of locally based services versus centrally controlled services, and the needs of the whole family, rather than the specific troubles of individual members of the family.

By giving the client and the worker equal status in developing a plan of treatment and help, LESFU implies that the current child welfare system is itself the cause of many of the problems of those enmeshed in it. LESFU seeks to divert children from the existing system and to demonstrate the potential of a different structure of child welfare services.

In analyzing such a range of issues, this book focuses on three different approaches to policy and program analysis—studies of process, performance, and product.

Process studies are concerned with understanding the relationships among the various governmental, political, and other organized interests in society that affect policy and program formulation. Usually case studies, "Process studies generally deal with such questions as the societal context in which programmatic decisions are made, the behaviors, motivations, and goals of the various actors who participated in the process, and the stages in which a program was developed. From this vantage point, a study of the LESFU would be a study of the power and influence of various organized groups related to the LESFU program. Such a study would be a political history of the project" (Gilbert and Specht, 1974, pp. 10–11).

A performance study of LESFU emphasizes its impact as well as the degree to which the program was actually carried out. Research techniques used in social science provide the major technical and theoretical knowledge and skill. Outcome measures are developed and a variety of quantitative and qualitative data collected in order to determine the degree to which the five distinguishing characteristics of LESFU noted earlier were realized. A performance study of LESFU emphasizes results.

A third type of study, product, stresses the values, theories, and assumptions that underpin LESFU. What programmatic options were considered, which others were unrecognized? The focus here is on choice. According to Gilbert and Specht (1974), LESFU's planning can be viewed as a series of choices among principles or guidelines that determine the benefits offered, to whom they are offered, how they are delivered, and how they are financed.

Why a particular alternative was chosen is the key question. Each aspect of LESFU's program is analyzed on the basis of the range of alternatives, the social values that lend support to each of these alternatives, and the theories or assumptions about human behavior or programs implicit in these alternatives.

The "why" of the alternatives chosen may be related to the power of various interest groups, professional values, or the need for the organization to cope with its environment. The choice may reflect a desire to use the latest ideas and techniques of service delivery or the necessity to give preeminence to a particular value, such as fairness or equity. This type of analysis focuses on the product of an administration's planning and management.

For example, Meld (1977), in a comprehensive and particularly perceptive analysis, notes that services integration is presently not so much an end to reach by technique as it is a process by which various interest groups try to achieve particular goals that have value for them. Such goals include improved capacity of agencies and programs to increase the quantity, quality, availability, and accessibility of services; better program control and system management, often in cost savings and increased cost effectiveness; greater equity and control over service resources in a given community, as in citizen participation or community control; and enhanced ability of individuals, families, and groups for personal and social activities.

These goals are not necessarily congruent; the pursuit of one may result in tension and strain with those who pursue another. Certainly, different groups have different concerns and focus these concerns on various targets in service-integration projects. For example, specialists, whether they be clinical social workers or vocational rehabilitation counselors, are unlikely to favor extensive coordination and integration of services if this means the loss of their professional identity. They are more interested in interagency coordination but not in vertical integration, where they risk control by a central authority. As Gage (1976) notes, specialists are likely to oppose the approach of the generalist case manager, who may be viewed as threatening the valued worker-client relationship or as having an assembly-line approach—inhuman and mass-production oriented. Program evaluators and managers focus on issues of efficiency and control. They may advocate information and reporting systems, sound accountability, cost benefit analysis, and needs assessment surveys. Unlike their generalist counterparts, who may share their enthusiasm for coordination and integration, they may suggest reduction in aggregate services levels to further integration. The evaluators and managers focus more on management reform than on program substance, thereby underplaying questions of service content in favor of structural organization questions (Kahn, 1976). Thus, professional orientations, values, and goals affect the course and direction service-integration projects take. These value conflicts are seldom, if ever, highlighted in agencies' public statements.

"The problem was not a complete absence of assistance, but rather a management problem: the failure to provide help in an effective and consistent manner, including a failure to stay with families to ensure that services were integrated around family need. Often hard-pressed, marginal families were expected somehow to relate the conflicting goals of diverse social workers representing different agencies, unable to coordinate their own efforts. The absence of any agency willing and able to coordinate, monitor, and focus the area's fragmented services on the needs of vulnerable families is one of the major factors leading to the development of the Lower East Side Family Union" (Schuman, 1976, p. 35). This direct statement belies a much more complicated reality.

****************** **2** ********************

Planning a New Model
for Integrating Services
and Preventing
Family Break-Up

****

Planning usually begins with a problem that someone feels must be overcome. Enarson (1975, p. 27) suggests that there are two planning models for solving problems—the Cook's Tour model and the Lewis and Clark model: "The Cook's Tour defines a precise schedule on a well-defined route; it moves in orderly progression amid known landmarks. The aim is to plan to avoid contingencies; the unexpected is to be avoided; all is schedule, order, routine. The Lewis and Clark model assumes that there is not enough knowledge to plan intelligently for all contingencies. Its virtue lies in the fact that it knows its goal, it knows where it wants to go. There are plans for general contingencies—building of campfires, fording of streams, delicate negotiations with the Indians. Success is a triumph of small daily successes—all within the context of a goal and a clear sense of direction."

The planners of LESFU followed the Lewis and Clark model. They defined the problem, delineated an approach to its solution, specified several techniques of offering service, and set up some procedures for dealing with unanticipated contingencies. Presumably, if Lewis and Clark had not known where they wanted to go, their expedition would have failed. Similarly, in social planning two key questions are "Is the problem adequately defined?" and "What are we concerned about?" Frequently in social programs the problem is defined too narrowly or too broadly. Sometimes the problem is confused with the solution.

Problem Definition

The process of problem definition is not easy to describe. Individuals' values affect what they view as social problems. Knowledge about and attitudes toward particular situations affect perspectives. To know how a situation became defined as a social problem, the people making the definition must be understood. Not everyone in a society recognizes a social problem at the same moment, as the civil rights movement of the 1950s and 1960s demonstrated.

Those who recognize a problem early and offer a solution are clearly the instigators of action. The ideas, motivations, and aspirations of these instigators always affect their plan for solving problems. The main instigators of LESFU were all directors of settlement houses in New York City's Lower East Side. Their agencies had a long history of serving immigrant populations, beginning around the turn of this century when the area was predominantly Jewish. By the 1970s, the population had shifted and the settlements were primarily serving a Hispanic, Black, and Oriental clientele.

The Lower East Side has perhaps the longest slum neighborhood history of any area in the country. Most of the tenement housing in its mile-square area is substandard and in disrepair. Alcoholism, drug addiction, and crime are rampant. Large families, poor health, unemployment, and underemployment are more the norm than the exception. At the same time, the area is a homeland for each of its minority groups, a neighborhood with its own traditions, where a foreign language may be the common tongue and where the accepted customs, loyalties, and hostilities may diverge from or directly oppose those of society outside (Heifetz, 1969). The settlement house directors were constantly adjusting their agencies' programs to cope with the complexity of this society.

Henry Rue, of the Harold Street Settlement, took the lead in urging the directors to face the problem of family disintegration in the area. Rue is not an ordinary executive of a social agency. He has a long career in government and national social agencies. During the War on Poverty of the 1960s he served on a variety of planning organizations and directed perhaps the most prominent antipoverty agency in the country. Personally gregarious, his administrative style is expansive. All of the organizations he headed during his career prospered under his tutelage and expanded their budgets two- and threefold.

In a field where money is always a source of anxiety and charisma is scarcer than money, he had both. In the early 1970s, as one of his many activities, Rue served as chairman of the board of the Citizens' Committee for Children (CCC)', a powerful pressure group concerned with the welfare of children in New York City.

The committee began during the Second World War with an interest in daycare and gradually expanded its focus to all types of services for children. Its power rests on its alliance of wealthy political power with academic and professional expertise. It is in the classic mold of a "good government" group, stressing planning, rationality, accountability, and responsibility.

In 1971, the Citizens' Committee issued its report, *A Dream Deferred,* an exposé of the past twenty-five years of child welfare crisis in New York City. This document both defines the problems of child welfare services and offers a direction for their solution.

> The public welfare system has been organized around two major tasks in New York City as in most American communities: (1) to provide financial assistance for those who are eligible and (2) to arrange temporary, long-term, and permanent placement of children. The latter task has been mislabeled "child welfare." Efforts in recent years to expand the goal of child welfare to include prevention of the need for placement have been half-hearted, small-scale, and ineffective. The situation will not be remedied unless the city faces a fundamental organizational defect; an organization built around the process of child placement cannot be expected to create programs and policies which emphasize promoting the welfare of children while they live at home in

their communities. Preventing the conditions which cause family break-up is the problem that must be solved, not the temporary crisis of insufficient placements for children.

We know that families cannot function without money, food, housing, jobs, or medical care. These are the fundamentals of family life. The community must not offer counseling, guidance, placement or treatment as substitutes for basic protection. Social services are misused unless they are a part of a complete social program.

Having made this statement, the committee then spells out a comprehensive service program.

What the Citizens' Committee offered was a total restructuring of the public social services. It proposed organizing this service system around the mission of helping families stay together and cope with emergencies. Rue was concerned and aware of the fact that, as of July 1971, the Department of Social Services would begin separating eligibility determination in public assistance from the provision of social services. The opportunity was present, in his view, to unify the previously fragmented social services, "those reserved for welfare recipients, and those for many others—into the most efficient and effective system which can be designed within the limits of resources and statutory requirements" (Citizens' Committee for Children, 1971, p. 21).

A Dream Deferred was a political document designed to influence the reorganization of the Department of Social Services. "The objective in any case should be the assignment of primary responsibility (in cases where people need help, support, guidance, counseling, substitute care, treatment) to locally based general family service social workers. They will work from the neighborhood offices of a reorganized Department of Social Services. And they will be outposted by the Department in schools, settlement houses, health stations, hospitals, housing projects, and so on. This staff will work closely with new locally based services and community corporations and other local groups, with the traditional voluntary sector and new voluntary agency programs, and with more specialized public programs" (1971, p. 23).

The key to the committee's plan is the family social worker, a professional responsible for seeing that immediate and long-term assistance is given to clients. The family social worker has the same relationship to families served as does the traditional, medical general practitioner. General family social workers give all of the service they are qualified to give without requiring the knowledge or prerogatives of a specialist. They are the center of case accountability and service integration, as *A Dream Deferred* suggested.

A crucial element of the plan outlined in *A Dream Deferred* is an array of services, a network of public utilities and public services that the general worker can assist families in securing: homemakers and homehelpers; meal delivery; referral or intervention to assist or improve emergency housing; daycare or other daytime child development services; medical care; registration for job training; help with problems of eligibility for financial aid; case work or group treatment to cope with handicaps or life crises; courses or individual help related to consumer issues; apartment furnishings; and information on nutrition, budgeting, family life adjustments, and drug abuse. The total service network needs access points—information centers or services, case-finding programs, and case advocacy services—that inform people of their rights, advise them, tell them what is available, and direct them to concrete service programs or to general family social workers, the entry point to helping services.

Public services and public responsibility form a third important aspect of the Citizens' Committee plan. A later document of CCC (1975, pp. 19–20) states, "While CCC recognizes that arrangements for purchasing services on a selective basis are necessary in any comprehensive system, history has demonstrated that a municipality that relies on purchased service without a public capacity to provide that service—a public presence capable of defining needs and assuring accountability—inevitably becomes a hostage of the providers, and there is then little or no effort to change or improve the quality of purchased services."

Although there are to be locally based services, with a family focus and with centralized public responsibility, nevertheless, there is a place for the voluntary agency. "When new programs are needed, competitive bidding might be encouraged, to clarify whether voluntary or commercial agencies, profit-making or nonprofit, can deliver a program more effectively for less cost than a direct city operation.

In child care, local access is a major factor, and community compatibility often important. Planning might at times specify that, if possible, the contract be written with a community corporation or a newly created local social agency. Stand-by emergency local shelter space in neighborhood homes, homemaker services, day care, are examples of such services" (Citizens' Committee for Children, 1971, p. 31).

The implications of this statement were certainly not lost on Rue. In addition, he was aware of the CCC's (1971, p. 25) recommendation:

> The change would be most apparent in what is now called child welfare; people with problems which now lead to Special Services for Children of the Department of Social Services or to the foster care divisions of various voluntary agencies would instead be guided to general family social workers. Because most contacts would be made earlier, the emphasis would be on striving to sustain the family through community-based help. Only if such efforts showed that child placement was essential for any period of time would the contact with the child placement specialists be made. The client served would have access to child placement specialists as needed, but child placement would be assumed to be avoidable or brief, unless there were proof to the contrary. Child placement would always be considered one of the possible services within the broader system. The lesson of the past is clear; child placement as a first resort for troubled families vitiates any attempt to cope with family and child problems; organizational autonomy for child placement services throws a service system off balance.

Rue knew that a report, no matter how widely circulated or intelligently written, does not by itself lead to action. Several key resources are needed to develop a program: information; expertise about substantive areas, such as child welfare; and, most importantly, sanction—the right to plan and develop a program. Rue had all three of these resources and the know-how to orchestrate them. In the spring of 1971, as chairman of the Director's Committee of the Lower East Side Settlements, he introduced the idea of developing a locally based service network, primarily for children but optimally to include all those in need of service. This group gave him the sanction to go forward.

To suggest a program that has as its core the coordination of services, Rue needed a sanctioning group larger than his own settlement; the Settlement Director's Group was ideal. On April 6, 1971, he submitted "A Planning Proposal for the Lower East Side Family and Children's Service" to the director of the New York City Human Resources Administration. This proposal informed the commissioner that a model was being developed on the Lower East Side that might be of use to him in any subsequent reorganization of public services. Although not directly stated, Rue clearly positioned the new model to take advantage of any change in public service delivery. The ostensible reason for submitting the proposal was merely to ask for the commissioner's response and general interest in playing a part in the coordination of services.

Rue stated the purpose of the agency and its basic philosophy as a community-based child welfare agency. In addition, he outlined the basic elements of the model, including teams of professionals and neighborhood residents, the concept of a general practitioner in social welfare, and the need to ensure service integration. He forecasted that the agency would develop into a general social service agency acting as an entry point to a variety of specialized services with the general practitioner accountable for integration of services and follow-through. The possibility of the agency subcontracting with other agencies for certain services and acting as an intermediary between the public and private sector was specifically indicated. Early intervention and community involvement at all phases of decision making were signaled.

In the very first planning proposal for the Lower East Side Family and Children's Service, most of the basic issues of social welfare policy with which the Family Union model would grapple were already identified: (1) decentralization of services; (2) service delivery—teams, professional standards, general practice; (3) family-support service systems; (4) community involvement; (5) career ladders for community residents and paraprofessional training, including university ties; and (6)' public-private relationships through contracts.

Certain factors that later became central to the Family Union plan were not explicitly mentioned in this early document— the ethnic orientation of the teams and the intention of forming a union of families. However, both were in line with the commitment indicated in the initial document to true community responsiveness.

Values and Assumptions

How a problem is defined affects its solution. Is family break-up the result of inequality and social disorganization or is it the result of personal inadequacy and neurosis? Problems are defined by the knowledge, values, preferences, and assumptions of those who offer solutions.

The planners of LESFU defined family break-up as primarily the result of inadequate community support in such areas as employment and housing and inadequate provision and coordination of services, such as counseling, homemaker, and health care. As directors of settlement houses, they had good reason for these beliefs; daily they dealt with families desperately in need of services, such as the following:

> Joan, a mother of six, walked reluctantly into a family-service agency. She had finally decided that she was too ill and too poor to take proper care of her four-year-old child, who had cerebral palsy and spinal meningitis. The strain of having to carry him up and down three flights of stairs several times a day was too much for her. She had decided he would have to be placed in an institution.
>
> She and her six children were living in a one-bedroom, rat-infested apartment that was often without heat and hot water. Joan had separated from her alcoholic husband, and was dependent on public assistance. She suffered from asthma and the aftereffects of a gynecological operation.
>
> The mother and her children were very close and

wanted to stay together. The children were helpful and
well adjusted, except for low reading and math scores at
school. Joan had tried to get help from several traditional
service agencies in the past, but they had failed to improve her situation [Bush, 1977, p. 49].

Besides a belief that services are inadequately delivered, social
workers usually believe that it is crucial to involve clients such as
Joan in setting up programs for their benefit. An obvious reason for
such involvement is the avoidance of needless errors or omissions.
Other social workers argue that involvement of clients is a democratic right, whether fruitful to the program or not. And others
insist that involvement is psychologically beneficial to clients, lessen-
ing feelings of alienation, dependency, and helplessness.

The actual results of involving clients in planning have been
mixed. When clients served on planning boards, they often were
overwhelmed by the sophistication and expertise of nonclient participants. Other problems related to the lack of representativeness of
clients—they often did not represent an organized constituency.
They were merely typical of a class, that is, aged or Black, but not
elected by peers. Yet, without client input, it is likely that programs
will be poorly constructed (Mayer and Timms, 1970).

LESFU was initially developed with little client input, but it
was designed to operate with a maximum of client control. As members of the board, they could alter the program once it was started.
Joint participation of individual clients and workers in setting service
goals was a cornerstone of LESFU's helping process. Clients were to
influence community policy toward child welfare through the union
of families. LESFU's planners accepted the psychological, political,
and programmatic arguments for client involvement. Since the
specifics of the service model had to be operationalized, there was
considerable opportunity for client involvement in program planning.

Another dilemma of planning involves the sanction or right
to plan. Many programs are controversial; if those who oppose a
program are brought into the planning process, conceivably a program could never start if the opponents could not be co-opted.
Usually this risk is avoided and programs begin with limited sanction.

LESFU was a rather uncontroversial program. Few people
object to trying to keep families together. The planning years were

relatively serene, especially because the planning instigators were all social workers. The original plan includes minimal discussion of school, church, and work organizations; few of these organizations were involved in the planning of LESFU. Planning by one profession risked insularity and postponed controversy until the program was operational. Yet, as will be shown, the program was launched with a good deal of support.

One final aspect of the LESFU plan deserves mention, in light of its limited sanction. Close to the heart of good government groups, such as the settlement directors, lies the idea of rationality and cooperation. Everyone supports the abstract idea of coordination, like the ideas of truth and justice. In reality, coordination inevitably means a measure of control over some people by others. A program started with limited sanction to coordinate can expect problems as control issues materialize. In the LESFU plan, the general family social worker has the responsibility to coordinate others. Although it may be necessary to have control vested in one person or group and to have the social workers, by virtue of their particular expertise, carry out this function, the person in this coordinating role is one with considerable power and status. It is doubtful that this fact will be lost on those to be coordinated—schoolteachers, policemen, union personnel, doctors, nurses, psychologists, and rehabilitation counselors—or that they will easily acquiesce to it. Sophisticated theories for dealing with this and other problems that have plagued coordination projects are required.

Summary

LESFU was not solely created by Henry Rue. Several other extremely competent and capable social workers devoted their time and effort to the project. With Rue, they shared a common value system and sense of purpose and gave support and stability to the agency during its formative years. They shared the belief that unnecessary placement of children should be prevented. They also saw services integration not as a fixed technique but as a process for reducing unnecessary placement.

Perhaps the key to understanding why the planning for the organization took the form it did lies in the fact that its founders confronted daily the tragedies and waste of family breakdowns. The desire for action, to do something, has been a source of both great strength and occasionally weakness in social welfare planning; actions can be taken before consequences are fully understood. Equally important goals can be selected that are not mutually reinforcing and may be antagonistic to each other.

Similarly, social work values have always given strength to the field. Yet, there are sometimes conflicts as to which value or values are superordinate. In services integration projects, which goals and which values are more important? Meld (1977, p. 94) suggests some of the considerations and their values: "The completeness of the array of services (values: adequacy, availability, accessibility)? The removal of institutional and structural barriers (value: institutional and system change)? System effectiveness (value: policy and program management and control)? Or increasing the capacities of individuals and groups to express and achieve their needs (value: personal and social functioning)?"

Could adequate and accessible services result in cost savings? Would increased citizen participation result in the improved capacity of agencies to deliver services? Would system change result in increased agency capacity to deliver services? These and other value and goal conflicts were in the background as the LESFU planners sought to secure funds to finance the program.

3

Setting Policy:
Fund Raising,
Community Participation,
and Client Selection

Simply defined, *policy* is a statement of who is to get what how. Gilbert and Specht (1974) suggest that social welfare policies may be seen as choices among principles or guidelines to determine what benefits are to be offered to whom, how these benefits are to be delivered, and how they are to be financed.

May 1972 to May 1974 constitutes the time of policy formulation at the LESFU. In May 1972, the first records of an organized board appeared; by May 1974, the first team leader and secretary had been hired. During 1972 the board was expanded from the original five directors of the Lower East Side settlements to include the director of the local hospital and the director of a church-oriented settlement house. In addition, two key members were added to the Family Union.

Judith Ash was the executive director of the Citizens' Committee for Children when its major report, *A Dream Deferred,* appeared. Her role as a consultant to the LESFU board gave credence to the project and was instrumental in achieving a grant from the Foundation for Child Development for exploring the feasibility of and for planning a neighborhood-based children and family service. Ash subsequently became a staff social science consultant to this foundation. This grant enabled the board to hire its first full-time worker to oversee the initial planning and operation of LESFU.

Sunnie Gold, who had worked for Rue in several capacities in prior years, became the chief consultant. At public meetings, she invariably spoke forcefully and with feeling about the plight of children in foster care. She was a mother and passionately committed to the rights and needs of minority children. Having a Black, female, and professionally trained social worker as chief consultant was a valuable factor in giving LESFU legitimacy in the community and the private foundations that provided most of the financial support during the planning years.

With the hiring of Gold, outreach efforts to the community grew. She began a campaign to touch base with all the major local and citywide agencies concerned with child welfare. By June 1972, Gold was a member of the Citizens' Committee task force on services to children, and she was beginning to meet with state and city officials on related activities on behalf of LESFU.

For this two-year policy and planning period, Rue served as chairman of the board, as well as executive director of LESFU temporarily. The board meetings with executives of the local settlements and agencies were used mainly as corrective tools to change and alter, advise and consent, and legitimate and sanction. The main planning was done by Rue in consultation with Ash and Gold. Too much time elapsed between the monthly meetings to take advantage of various opportunities for funding and development. Thus, even in a very small organization, such as LESFU, there was an inner elite. Part of this may have resulted from Rue's style, which was to move quickly and take advantage of opportunities, rather than to wait and secure the participation and involvement of all interested parties. The connection between fund raising and LESFU's policy of services and service delivery was kept quite close

during the planning period; this connection grew out of the sophistication and experience of the board members.

Funding

Rue was keenly aware that the first crucial issue for
LESFU was funding to begin operation. In his mind, it was less
important to spell out the actual operations of LESFU than to
remain flexible in approaching funding sources in order to secure
their funds. He was willing to change approaches but was not willing to compromise the essence of LESFU—decentralization of child
welfare services and accountability for services rendered. As a pro-
curer of funds, Rue has few peers. His skill is based on a number of
talents, including knowing when to compromise. He had a clear
view of what it would take to make LESFU viable. He felt that the
program could not succeed on private funds alone. During two years
of gaining the support of private foundations, he never lost sight of
the fact that ultimately a public commitment must be secured for
LESFU. Rue considered the purpose of LESFU was to demonstrate
a new way of providing public child welfare services.

During the planning period, annual commitments of from
$15 to $50 thousand were secured from seven different foundations;
many of these foundations contributed for two to three years. In
some ways pyramiding multiple funding sources is a mirage, but by
involving the government in an attempt to show private foundations
that continued funding of the program after a year or two is possible
and by showing the government that private foundations with their
own staff consultants consider a project worthy of funding, Rue was
able to use the resources of one group to entice another to provide
funds.

A brief review of LESFU's early funding efforts will illustrate Rue's approach. The original 1971 planning proposal anticipated that the organization could receive the same per capita per
diem payment for child care from the state that was available to
citywide child welfare organizations. The organization was basically
conceived of as a quasi-governmental unit depending on public
funds and providing a demonstration of how a community-con-

trolled organization can be responsive both to its own constituency and to a citywide governmental organization.

Notwithstanding the interest in public funding, in the early spring of 1973, the Family Union received a planning grant from the Foundation for Child Development for organizing and studying the possibility of the neighborhood-based children and family service. Soon Rue moved from city organizations to private foundations. However, minutes of the earliest board meetings show that consideration was given early to cooperation with a large private foundling home, as well as with the city probation department. At one meeting, Earl Greenstreet, the director of a local settlement, Collegiate House, suggested paying parents out of state funds to act as foster parents for their own children. At a meeting of the steering committee two months later, the idea of city staff being stationed in LESFU was discussed with a representative of the Department of Social Services on the Lower East Side.

Flexibility in program ideas, as well as in funding sources, was the hallmark of this planning period. A variety of proposals were sent out over the years; some of them involve inconsistencies caused by the fact that they were created to fit into the programs and purposes of the funding sources. For example, a proposal sent to the State Department of Social Services had a larger staff—five social worker associates, three homemakers and housekeepers—and more teams than were immediately anticipated and a larger administrative structure than was later thought feasible. The Family Union also applied for federal monies under child abuse funding provisions but did not intend to change its basic approach; such funding would have been used in line with LESFU program to the greatest extent possible.

Another example of the flexibility of LESFU relates to its prevention priorities. The original planning proposal embodied both the narrower focus of preventing placement and the larger concept of enhancing family development. Title IV (A and B) funds were available for prevention; if the Family Union could agree on a suitable definition of preventive care and convince the city and state to accept it, they could tap these resources as well. But LESFU never clearly defined, as will be shown, what it really meant by prevention until early in 1975, partly because the openness of the definition aided fund raising. The problems of defining *prevention* in the years to come proved quite difficult.

The correctness of Rue's strategy was proven. His personal contacts and reputation not only succeeded with the private foundations, they also succeeded with the state. In the fall of 1974, a new governor, Hugh Carey, was elected. Carey sought to develop, during his campaign, position papers on social welfare. Rue was active in his campaign and shortly after the governor's election, he and Judith Ash headed the governor's task force on social services. They were presumed to have the governor's ear and considerable influence with him; this contact was not lost on other state bureaucrats.

When decisions were finally made in late 1975 on the programs the state would fund under Title IV–B for preventive programs, small, unknown LESFU—in comparison to large sectarian federations and agencies with powerful boards and contacts—was able to hold its own and received $500 thousand from the state. Even with the state, a good idea plus a reputation for competence and personal contacts carried the day. In addition to Rue's contacts, Ash had statewide contacts of her own, both professional and personal. However, these contacts should not be overemphasized. LESFU offered something new, presented the possibility of a cheaper and more effective service, and merited its own funding, especially since many of the other programs were merely old programmatic ideas increased in cost and size, with nothing really new.

One other important variable in fund raising to note is information. Rue was knowledgeable not only about the potential of public and private systems but also about their failings and limitations. He had diligently pursued city sources and written proposals for Title IV–B funds only to find, after a year of meetings after meetings and calls after calls, that the city was not aware that deadlines and specific guidelines had been issued. At one point, no one in the city even knew where to find the proposal that Rue had sent.

Granting the need for more efficiency, it seems nevertheless that there should be better and more efficient ways for government and foundations to discover and develop innovative and creative service delivery programs. Broad and vague definitions of prevention and innovation in proposals do not provide much guidance. In such situations, reputations for competence, as well as personal contacts, inevitably play a greater role than they would in more defined program areas. Rue was able to turn this weakness to LESFU's gain. LESFU was certainly a spectacular success in terms of fund raising, but the necessary preoccupation with fund raising deflected the organization from planning its services and delivery system.

Program Design

Many of the members of the board had been deeply involved in the poverty program of the 1960s as both administrators and service providers. If anything, this program was the gray eminence of LESFU, yet it left as many programmatic questions unanswered as answered.

Clearly the board was aware of some of the limitations and potentials of the new modes of service delivery pioneered during the 1960s. They also, especially Rue, were aware of some of the basic contradictions that emerged between the needs of clients and the maintenance needs of social agencies.

Many poverty agencies faced the problem of securing financial support from public sources while trying to maintain their own independence and ability to confront the same institutions on which their support depended. This problem, according to Rue, could be eliminated if an agency was truly a voluntary association, free from dependence on public funds, thus capable of controversial social actions.

On August 8, 1972, the Lower East Side Family and Children Services changed its name to the Lower East Side Family Union. Representing more than just a name change, from this point onward the Family Union was considered not one but two organizations—a service agency and a membership organization. The Union of Families was designed to be a truly voluntary organization, related to, but separate from, the service agency that sponsored it. This freed the union to engage in controversial activities, to agitate and advocate a variety of changes in the public social welfare program. Its budget could not be threatened because it depended solely on private funds for its financing.

Subsequent chapters examine the actual experience of the

union in realizing these goals. In inception the Family Union, with its emphasis on a voluntary union, joined a voluntary association to a quasi-public one in order to overcome a problem clearly demonstrated earlier—it is impossible for a public agency to provide funds and then be subjected to the criticism of those it funded.

Significantly, the exact relationship between the union and the service organ of LESFU was not clearly defined during the planning years. Members would be recruited into the union, but what the criteria of membership would be and what staff would be required to organize the union were unasked questions. Presumably they would be answered when the union was operationalized.

Yet another problem clearly articulated in the poverty program of the 1960s was the difference between the rhetoric and the reality of community participation. Was the intent of community participation to change participants, their views of themselves, and their ability to participate? Or was community involvement meant to mobilize the power of people to achieve specific ends, no matter whether people were changed in the process or not? And whatever the intent, did people really wish to participate? This argument over the ends and means and the extent of community participation was never fully resolved in the poverty program. As will be noted later, LESFU continued to be plagued by the same dilemma in its efforts to establish a union of families.

Another common criticism of the poverty program was the inability to determine what effect any particular remediation or counseling program had on poverty and its incidence. The LESFU planners, aware that the favorable political climate of the middle and late 1960s had disappeared and that now social agencies are called to account for costs and benefits, determined early to devise a program that would be amenable to objective evaluation. Of course, the beauty of the creation of two organizations was that the union could engage in a variety of activities that, given their nature, could not be subject to the same type of analysis.

Still another problem that plagued the poverty program was its failure to define precisely the criteria of eligibility for service. What makes a person poor? Who is a delinquent? In addition to the substantive problems of defining poverty or delinquency were community relations problems. One large poverty agency, which determined that its job training program would be opened only to those with a criminal record, was picketed by a group of adolescents holding signs that said "Do we have to rob a store to get a job?"

Rue and others on the board were keenly aware that if the definition of prevention of placement was vague and open, LESFU would soon be swamped with service requests. An open definition would leave LESFU in the position of being a neighborhood service center for all the various problems of the people of the Lower East Side. A high percentage of these families have children and extremely serious personal problems. All such families could very easily be defined as in danger of having to place their children outside the home.

The disagreement over whether LESFU should serve only those who might be referred to Special Services for Children (SSC) for placement or all problem-ridden families was the first evidence of a difference of opinion between the board and the staff. Gold, the chief consultant and only staff member during most of the planning period, had the responsibility of contacting the community and developing a plan for letting individual families know of the LESFU service. She felt a strong commitment to serving the poor of the community. Along with Gold, the first team leader, hired in 1974, would have to bear the burden of explaining to people why they would be denied service even though they had desperate problems unrelated to their children. They resisted this task. At issue was whether LESFU was a demonstration project or a service project—the same issue that haunted aspects of the poverty program.

The antipoverty effort was also interested in institutional change. Poverty agencies often quite consciously took an adversarial and confrontational position against existing social agencies, viewed as the targets of change. Although the results of the adversary stance of poverty agencies were mixed, it was clear to Rue and others that the total climate in the country that supported such a stance had changed. The decision to design LESFU in a cooperative model was strongly related to the ethos of the early 1970s—rationality, accountability, and cost effectiveness.

Early in 1974 at a meeting of community agencies, including representatives of SSC, Rue was angrily upbraided by a member of the Social Service Workers Union: "You are going to be doing just what we are currently doing; in that sense your program is wasteful." Rue adroitly answered this attack by noting that LESFU did not intend to duplicate services but was an additional resource for SSC to use whenever it saw fit. The agency's main objectives were resource development, referral, and case management.

Of all the functions of LESFU, case accountability is the most crucial. To achieve it, LESFU developed the family service contract, which would be written for each client, clearly stating the client's needs and what services would be offered. The contract would be signed by the client, a LESFU representative, and the agencies that offered services. Rue, Greenstreet, and others on the board were keenly aware that such contracts could become merely formal shams if there were no enforcement procedure. They felt enforcement would occur by virtue of the fact that the executives of all the participating agencies would be members of the board of directors of LESFU. It is unclear whether this idea developed out of a discussion of the problems of enforcing contracts or as a pragmatic and intuitive response to the actual situation, where the settlement houses initially provided the majority of services and were represented on the board by their executives. At a board meeting in late 1975, when a new agency was suggested for membership, Greenstreet clearly stated that the executive must be told that attendance is expected at board meetings and that stand-ins are not acceptable.

Similarly, considerable effort during the planning years was spent in interpreting the agency and family service contracts for the staffs of the local settlement houses. Toward the end of the planning period, when LESFU began referring community residents for service, the staff was encouraged to meet with staffs of other agencies to develop cooperative services prior to the development of formal contracts between the agencies and LESFU.

Although these early relationships did not always run smoothly, in 1975, when the first general contracts were signed between LESFU and the agencies concerning basic terms of their relationship, no agency executive refused to sign. It is unlikely, given the resistance in subsequent years, that these signings would have occurred so smoothly if the agencies' staffs had more power to

say yes or no. Yet the significant fact is that the agencies signed
and that their executives were committed to the project. Subsequent
chapters will explore the problems that ensued because the staffs of
the participating agencies were not involved in the decision to sign.

LESFU profited from another experience of the poverty
program. The antipoverty effort had begun with a great deal of
rhetoric about the poor and analysis based on class, but experience
soon demonstrated that ethnicity was an extremely important variable. Community organizations tended to develop along ethnic and
religious lines; clients, at least initially, tended to gravitate to those
who appeared similar to them. Partly for service reasons and partly
out of a desire to be accepted by the clients and the community,
LESFU organized itself along ethnic lines. The three teams were
each built on ethnic differences—the first team was composed of
Spanish speakers; the second was directed toward the Chinese
population, with all the team members Chinese; the third team was
tentatively oriented toward an area with a heavy concentration of
Blacks. The ethnic orientation of the first two teams was easily
justified by the necessity for a common language. But the board
began to raise questions. Harvey Cardinal, the director of the settlement Monroe House, was troubled by the fact that since Team Two
was wholly Chinese, members of other groups in the area might be
reluctant to seek service from this team; he had constituents from
many other groups, and his settlement house was situated in the area
covered by Team Two.

It was assumed that at some point a considerable number of
community residents would serve on the board of LESFU; presumably, these residents would represent ethnic groups. One of the
lessons of the 1960s' War on Poverty was that ethnic groups tended
to become involved in a variety of disputes when they were represented (Weissman, 1970). Ethnicity was a volatile factor in many
poverty programs, and it had its effects on LESFU. For example,
the board supposed it could be a forum for hammering out among
various groups mutual interests that transcend cultural and racial
lines. LESFU planned to have lay and professional members on the
board, although in the earlier poverty program, community residents
had difficulty participating on boards on an equal basis with highly
sophisticated professionals (Beck, 1969).

In contrast to the issue of enforcing contracts, where LESFU had developed a concept, the area of community participation on the board was not developed conceptually. What emerged, as Chapter Four shows, might have been anticipated.

Another problematic aspect of the poverty program was the hiring of so-called "indigenous workers" to staff social welfare programs. People who shared many of the problems that clients suffered from were hired to provide help, on the assumption that clients were more likely to relate to them, as well as to perform the tasks required in many jobs that did not require university and graduate education.

The experience with indigenous workers in the poverty program was mixed. On the one hand, they performed a variety of tasks; initially, at least, they did relate more easily with clients and often served as passionate advocators for clients' rights. On the other hand, they presented a variety of problems; they were insecure about their jobs and became quite organizationally conservative, naturally enough since they were unable to secure other jobs as easily as people with credentials. Incompetent workers were difficult to fire, because they tended to organize their neighbors and local residents to support them in any disagreement with the agency's administration. Suffering from many of the problems of the client population, they had more health, legal, and emotional problems than more affluent staff members. Agencies that hired these workers had to be prepared to offer a variety of services to them in order to maintain satisfactory work.

From the poverty program's experience, it was clear that training was required for most jobs in social agencies, but training did not necessarily have to occur in a university or formal school setting. It could be offered on the job but such training is expensive. Nevertheless, LESFU planned an extensive in-service program, which it continues to carry out. A key question remains, do indigenous workers provide the type and quality of service that compensate for the cost involved in hiring them? The poverty program did not provide a definite answer for the LESFU planners.

One final experience of the poverty program was important in planning LESFU. Many poverty programs organized themselves departmentally. An essential department in such programs was the

community organization department, which organized the con-
sumers or the clients of the agencies to press for needed institutional
and social changes. One criticism of such an organizational structure is that it often brought the agency into conflict with other
organizations with which it was simultaneously seeking cooperation.
Can a group both organize a rent strike and ask the same landlord
to cooperate in a housekeeping and sanitation program for the
neighborhood? The design of a separate community organization
department did not work for many poverty agencies, perhaps because an agency's total program can be viewed as community
organization. The administration must coordinate the programs of
the agency rather than allow various departments to pursue their
own specific ends (Weissman, 1969).

      To a certain extent the teams of LESFU were meant to
counter the problem of the relationship between social services and
community action. The origin of the teams lies in the old community
development concept, where teams of workers went from the central
government to local villages or districts of large cities. In LESFU,
teams were primarily composed of residents working in their own
community. The essence of the team approach lies in the virtue of
its smallness, which makes it less likely that specialization and de-
partmentalization will malfunction. Smallness helps to ensure that
everyone on the team works toward the same end.

      The original poverty program error of various departments
moving in opposite directions was avoided. The training offered in
LESFU was for the general social worker, not a caseworker, group
worker, or community organizer. In dealing with individual cases,
workers should see the opportunities for community action and feed
them back into the Family Union or develop programs through the
various teams. In some ways, this focus represents an earlier view of
social action by agencies: Caseworkers, through their case-by-case
experiences, develop ideas about clients' common problems, caused
by the existing society, and out of this common experience grow
policies and programs, which are presented to the general public
for enactment. This scheme for social action had not worked well
in prior decades nor did it work well at LESFU. The pressures of
too many clients, plus the lack of training and support for workers

to look at broader issues, were constraining factors. When these dilemmas emerged at LESFU, the lessons of the poverty program were partially forgotten and a community organization specialist was hired.

Summary

Gilbert and Specht (1974) propose that an organization develops its policy by studying the range of alternatives within each dimension, the social values that lend support to these alternatives, and the theories or assumptions implied in these alternatives. If policy making is a conscious systematic effort leading to choice, then clearly LESFU deviated from this process. The agency's planners fell back on their previous experiences, primarily in the poverty program, which organized their alternatives, values, theories, and assumptions. These experiences directed the planners' attention to certain problems and gave urgency to a desire to avoid past errors. The family service contracts were a creative extension of the simple one-agency/one-client contract. The LESFU service-provider agency contracts, in conception, were geared to avoid unnecessary confrontations, which often occurred in poverty programs.

In addition, although LESFU was in fact a funding tour de force, the financing of the program was always a source of concern, especially in the planning years. The decision to hire indigenous workers was probably made as much on the basis of cost as it was on the value of their language skills and ethnic knowledge. In such a financially pressured situation, especially when the planned program is complex and has multiple goals, planning on the basis of experience has two general drawbacks: it increases the likelihood that some decisions will be premature when additional searching for new theories and concepts might be advantageous, and it assumes that past experiences were understood.

The experiences of some aspects of the poverty program were not completely assimilated by the planners of LESFU, for example, community organization, board membership, and ethnicity. Similarly, a major theory of helping, *network therapy*—the organization of relevant friends, relatives, neighbors, other people to help a person or family in distress—was not given much consideration (Speck and Reuveni, 1969). This lapse proved important when the agency had considerable difficulty in organizing a union of families.

Initially, the agency did successfully avoid overplanning and allowed room for experimentation and innovation in its basic procedures. But in some ways LESFU was caught in a planning dilemma. What must be decided before a program becomes operational? What can be worked out in the process of operating a program? Over the years an answer emerged at LESFU that will become clear in subsequent chapters.

4

Defining
Staff Responsibilities
and Priorities

A program begins when a staff is hired and trained to carry out its procedures and activities; program means then become as crucial as program goals. Operationalizing the goals or explicating the means involves much more in an organizational context than determining specifically how services will be given. It involves developing communication and lines of authority within the agency, arranging departmental relationships, setting priorities, developing relationships with other organizations, and most importantly, training the staff to work effectively with clients and with other staff members.

The complexity of this task lends credence to Selznick's (1949, pp. ix–x) view that ideals evaporate when the compelling realities of organizational life are permitted to run their natural course: "Means tyrannize when the commitments they build up divert us from our true objectives. Ends are impotent when they are so abstract and unspecified that they offer no principles of criticism and assessment." The object of program development is to ensure that means do not tyrannize ends.

LESFU's operationalization phase began approximately in
May 1974 when the first group of workers was hired and extended
until March 1976 when the total staff was in place and working.
This period in its history was one of great achievement as well as
considerable difficulty. It is easy to pass over the achievements since
difficulties are often all too obvious. Yet the seeds of collapse of many
organizations are sown during their initial operating periods. As
planners pass the reins to implementors, confusion and controversy
over priorities inevitably result. But what is striking about LESFU
is that the essentials of the project were not forgotten, even though
the organization faced severe strain. The essential project elements
advocated (1) a neighborhood, rather than a central, base; (2)
preventive, rather than protective, action; (3) a family orientation;
(4) a target population in danger of breakdown (placement); (5)
integration of fragmented services; (6) provision for mutual decision
making by clients and workers; and (7) alteration of the public
human services system. How and why the organization maintained
its equilibrium is the subject of this chapter.

Means

Means can tyrannize ends for a variety of reasons. Sometimes
there is an emotional and historical connection to the means. Sometimes the means are much clearer than the ends, which are vague
and unmeasurable. In the best of programs, where there are a
variety of means or procedures, there are tensions; mechanisms are
needed to resolve those tensions.

The Tyranny of Money. Sarah Savant, a bright, analytical
social worker, had recently received a doctorate in social welfare.
Her interest was in policy analysis, and she was hired early in 1974
to be the social historian of LESFU, documenting and describing
the program's development. Shortly after her arrival, she was asked
by Henry Rue to assume the title of administrator and take over
much of the program's operation, only secondarily writing the social
history.

She had very little experience in supervision or organizational
management. Her job title was redefined because of questions raised

by a foundation about the administrative experience of Sunnie Gold, the chief consultant. Gold was a professor at a university, but her administrative experience was limited, at least in the eyes of the foundation. To placate this funding source, Rue switched titles. The foundation did not check into the credentials of Savant. Actually, Gold retained the title of chief consultant, but she was also the administrative superior and supervisor of Savant, the administrator, following the model of a hospital administrator and a medical director with the medical director the administrative superior.

This key change in personnel was made not because of the technical competence required to fulfill certain tasks but because of the need for funds. The results of this decision plagued LESFU for six months. The first problem was a severe disagreement between the new administrator and the chief consultant as to who was responsible for what.

Typical of the ambiguous authority in the union was the hiring process. Some of the members of the first team were hired by the chief consultant, others were hired by the administrator. An internal report gives some of the flavor of this confusion:

> The staff waited for Sunnie's arrival to resolve things; meanwhile the issues and conflicts would intensify with the passage of time. She [Sunnie] did not attend administrative meetings; therefore communication would take place on a one-to-one basis with her, rather than in an open group process. . . . even the clerical staff developed a tendency to wait for "big sister" to come down with the judgment.

> Aside from personality problems, there seemed to be more serious issues. Internally, the program was not taking any clear direction, but drifting. Despite all the talk about program development—formulating a membership, using a group model of practice, working with a whole family—there was little follow-through.

The creation of the jobs of consultant and administrator was more the result of fiscal necessities than rational planning in terms of the most effective administrative structure. As the quoted report indicates, the staffing patterns at the lower levels of the organization were similarly affected.

The central service mechanism of the Family Union was the team, whose core lay in community residents. These community residents would be called *social work associates, homemakers,* and *housekeepers.* Of the three, the social work associate was the most important. He or she was to be responsible for ensuring that clients got service from agencies with whom the union contracted.

Only the team leader was a professionally trained worker. At board level discussions, the point was made repeatedly that the union would be careful not to alter the professional/nonprofessional relationships on the team so radically as to endanger the primary activities of the local community resident, the front-line worker. This concept was not relaxed until the third team appeared in January 1976; it was comprised completely of city workers on loan to the agency. The union was unable to persuade the city to provide workers who were community residents.

In relation to the hiring of local residents, the experience of the 1960s was extremely mixed (Jones, 1969). The board was concerned with matters other than ways of handling emergent staff problems. In mid 1974, they did not have a commitment from the state to provide monies necessary to keep the program going for another year. Private foundation funds were still needed.

Perhaps the board assumed that the consultant and the administrator had certain skills, but a report written in December 1974 by Savant indicates they did not: "Among staff, signs of strains were building up during the last half of 1974 and became extremely visible just before Christmas. The team leader had actually been hired in late March and the two social work associates had come on in May; the clerk-typist and the homemaker were not hired until October. The team leader was constantly frustrated in her efforts to show development of the team, because in effect she had no team working for two months; the new homemaker had been sitting around with very little work for over six weeks." Finally, when a case was found for the homemaker, there were also problems fitting her work and role together with the front-line social work associate assigned to the case. The training problem in the team had reached a crescendo; the paperwork that the team members were responsible for was not getting done, partly due to delays caused by illness, partly because the two social work associates were inefficient in handling it.

One social work associate had an operation and illness in her family, the other associate had pneumonia. Thus, the team was rarely complete from the middle of October to the beginning of the new year. The consequences of this for morale, for training, and for work are obvious, as Savant noted: "Very few additional families were added to the union's clientele during this period, and plans for a membership drive and training were never put into practice. There was also considerable need for support for workers . . . by their fellow workers and by the administration. Indeed, the consultant stated that she tended to give therapeutic help to at least one of the workers at any hour she was called upon."

By the fall of 1974, the board began questioning the administrator and consultant about the activities of LESFU. In addition, critical reports were received from other settlements. Questions were raised about the original team leader's competence, since board members were often present when she presented LESFU to the staffs of their various agencies. As these problems surfaced, the second team leader was hired in November 1974, followed shortly by additional social work associates and homemakers. The board felt that the staff problems were individual problems of competence. No doubt they also felt they had few options because of financial constraints.

Yet money will always constrain staffing policies. Program designers cannot simply dismiss it as a sad fact of life. Options need to be developed for dealing with this constraint. The potentials and limits of each option must be spelled out. A means of monitoring the selected option must be created.

Perhaps the staff in charge of the fiscal planning cannot develop the staffing or program options, or vice versa, since each has its own pressures and constraints. A search for options may be foreclosed too soon when one set of pressures predominate. Tension between equally important activities may be necessary for effective decision making. At LESFU, the pressures of funding were not counterbalanced, and staffing decisions suffered as a result.

The Tyranny of Time. The consequences of such decisions

as changing job titles were not simply that the wrong personnel were hired; they were of a more subtle nature. LESFU was based on a new way of service delivery, yet, in staffing during this early period, personnel were hired as if the LESFU centers were actually one-stop neighborhood centers where a variety of services would be offered. Lip service was given to the new model, but initial hiring was not done on the basis of what skills were needed to operate within the confines of that model.

This situation is epitomized by the fact that one of the Puerto Rican social work associates had worked in an agency where his main function was to help clients get their entitlements from the Department of Social Services. He saw his job at LESFU in the same manner and saw nothing wrong with spending a day at the welfare office with a client. The concept of restricting intake to families in danger of having to place their children in foster care was foreign to him; if someone needed help he intended to give it. He also did not clearly see the necessity for working with other organizations to obtain their services; he was a provider and not a co-ordinator. Ultimately he was asked to resign but not without considerable strain in the organization.

This firing in the summer of 1975 was probably a crucial one for the organization's survival as a demonstration project. The agency's ability to withstand community pressure—calls from local politicians and vague rumors about racism—and to fire the worker signaled to other staff members that LESFU was committed to its basic concepts. The board's unanimity about the project's purpose helped make it possible to dismiss a local worker whose good intentions were counterproductive to the agency's ends. Many new projects flounder simply because they lack a strong and committed board to meet such crises.

Nevertheless, there seems to have been little anticipation of the difficulties of operationalizing various staff members' jobs. The assumption was that this process would be worked out as people were hired. The problem with this on-the-job planning is that when people are confronted with clients they develop their own perceptions of their roles. Thus, a good deal of confusion has to be overcome and a good deal of unlearning has to occur once their duties are clearly defined.

Some homemakers did more than help with the household chores and escort clients; the roles of the social work associates and the homemakers were unclear. The staff did not understand participation in a demonstration-research project, why only certain clients could be served, and why they could not provide certain services, which created a division between the staff (the implementors) and the board (the policy makers). Commitments grew under the pressure of meeting client needs. Why do we need contracts? Why do we need research? Why do we need a social history? Why do we need community organization? These questions reverberated through the staff and plagued the agency. The weak administrative structure that existed prior to 1976 could not provide the answers.

The Tyranny of Ideology. Sunnie Gold's annual report in 1973 recounts the board's beginning: "In the very first meeting of the core group of settlement house executives, following the hiring of a consultant, discussions got underway to ensure the presence of neighborhood people . . . at this decision-making level. Once the Family Union is incorporated and the program is operating with service teams in the health areas, plans will be set in motion for the election of members to the board of directors. . . . Two community representatives from each of the health areas being served will be elected to the governing board. Guidelines are currently being prepared to define membership in the Family Union and eligibility to vote in Family Union elections and to establish eligibility for board membership and . . . terms of office."

The report goes on to note that community residents were invited to work with the steering committee and the consultant. And to further this end, a group session was held to give community members an opportunity to get acquainted with each other and with the consultant, learn about the background of the Family Union, study issues before the steering committee, and explore together and question the role of the steering committee. According to the report, "this approach provided a useful bridge" between the community and the Family Union. Subsequently, community representatives have participated in public and private fund-raising efforts, meetings regarding incorporation and licensing, and other Family Union activities with conviction and effectiveness.

A report written in the summer of 1974 states "The first

election will be held in the fall of 1974. The Family Union board will be the policy-making board. In addition, as each health area direct service team is developed, it will have its own advisory board, which will elect representatives to the Family Union board of directors." Actually the situation was quite different than the report anticipated. Very few community members ever participated on the board of directors from 1974 to 1977. Only two community people, defined as neighborhood residents without a college education, attended regularly; they were employees of social agencies.

One reason why the community was not adequately represented lies in the ideological, rather than programmatic, nature of the union. As stated previously, the union was to be composed of clients, residents, and professionals in the neighborhood concerned about the welfare of children. The ideology of citizen participation is not easily questioned. Rue and the other directors were sincere in their desire to have community residents participate in the decision-making processes, but the first eighteen months of LESFU were devoted to securing the funds and establishing the organization. Few community residents, if any, knew of the various laws pending in the city council and state legislature or had contacts with foundations and expertise in fund raising. Their participation, although genuinely desired, was actually not needed for founding the organization.

Originally, the clients were to be well represented on the board; this proved impossible. Besides the obvious problem of the sophisticated level of knowledge required to participate on the LESFU board, the majority of clients were Spanish- and Chinese-speaking people. Participating at a board meeting dealing with complex issues was not something they could readily do when only English was spoken.

The problems of gaining community representatives on the board, as well as creating a union of clients, were subjects of frequent discussions at board meetings during 1975. In the fall of 1975, a consultant, a well-known expert on community organizations, was hired to develop a proposal for a client organization. The exact scope and function of this organization were left to the consultant, whose hiring symbolized the board's inability to cope with this problem.

Clearly, it was the idea of a family union that attracted several foundations. The family union was to be an organization of clients that would serve as an ongoing interest group or watchdog for children's services and as a source of mutual support and help for its constituent members.

What was missing in all the proposals' discussions about the family union was an operational statement—how it was to be started, what programs it would involve itself in, how it would relate to the service arm of LESFU, what its relationship would be with contracts, whether it would require additional staff or be the responsibility of all the teams, and a host of similar questions. The family union part of the program was merely an idea to be developed once it began operation. The team leaders, given all their other problems, tended to view the sketchiness of the union idea as a limitation in funding such a vague concept. Certainly their ability to conceptualize how a union of families could be organized was not part of their recruitment criteria.

The consultant produced an excellent analysis of the problems related to creating organizations comprised of low-income, problem-ridden members. The consultant suggested that a union should not be created before attempting to organize clients around specific projects, such as setting up group homes on the Lower East Side or trying to get remedial services for children. If these individual projects were successful, an organization could be formed from the members active in the individual projects. Later discussions with the team leaders concerning this proposal focused around how much staff time would be needed to help the community organize. The consultant suggested that a community worker would have to be hired. There was considerable discussion around whether a homemaker from each team would work full-time with the community organizer. To some measure, the team leaders' lack of enthusiasm was related to the fact that they were having difficulty developing the service strategy of LESFU, contracts, work agreements, and the like. Developing the union was simply too much work at that time.

What really hampered the board in operationalizing the union was their ideological commitment to citizen participation in policy making coupled with their desire to hire local residents. Neither of these commitments could be relinquished; as such the problem was not soluble. Using some volunteers, instead of paid workers, as well as initially limiting citizen participation to service provision rather than policy making might have helped.

There are certain types of services that volunteers, especially resident neighborhood volunteers, can provide (Speck, 1967). They are available at a variety of times, have numerous contacts and relationships with other people, and have access to needed resources in the neighborhood. Outreach—seeking out clients—escort, and homemaking are tasks they can easily perform. It may be that such tasks are the basis on which even more complex participation can be developed. The following example illustrates this possibility:

> In the course of the four-hour staffing, the real core of the [volunteer] lay therapy model became visible, as the workers recounted their efforts over the preceding two weeks with the two or three clients to whom they had each been assigned. While there is an ever-expanding list of activities which the lay therapist undertakes in an effort to help a client [such as providing information about available services and programs; providing on-the-spot counseling in marital relations, sex education, and child development; providing a parenting model; providing transportation or babysitting to enable the parent to attend Parents Anonymous (small therapy groups run by and for abusive and neglectful parents), or even supplying emergency funds for food], the workers prefer to think of their basic responsibility to their clients in terms of friendship—noncritical, nonjudgmental, nonpunitive friendship. It is this climate of support that was apparent in the staffing and that enables the client to transform a negative self-image, accept discipline alternatives to abuse, and ultimately to gain a level of stability and independence [Berkeley Planning Associates, 1976, pp. 121–122].

Ends

Ideology tyrannizes when options are blocked because the nature and direction of the ideology limits the search for alternative solutions. The possibility that hiring local residents would limit the development of the union was never considered. Similarly, ends are impotent when "good intentions" are the central criteria of goals. Goals are statements of intention, yet they lose a good deal of force when an organization has several goals, any one of which may conflict with another. Typical of this problem was LESFU's commitment to providing service as well as to adding to the knowledge of how to provide service. On many occasions the board had stated its commitment to both research and service.

Stanley Firestone, consultant to Gold and Savant, suggested a conceptual scheme for research—the goal attainment scale, which had been used in several social agencies. This scheme, in essence, is first a series of agreements made between the client and the worker to carry out specific tasks. Each task is expected to be completed by a specified date. Potential outcomes are attached to each task: the most favorable outcome, the expected outcome, and the least favorable outcome. The staff is then able to monitor progress with the clients. The goal attainment scale was never successful in 1974 and 1975; it was often talked about but nothing concrete ever occurred. As of December 1974, no forms had been filled out, despite the social work associates' promises that they would. A report by Savant illustrates a problem: "The meeting of December 5 began with difficulty: Only one social work associate was present, and he had not completed any forms prior to the meeting. Thereafter, the team leader showed considerable uncertainty about the nature of the forms and raised many of the same questions, which had been discussed months before. One of the social work associates became quite confused and declared, 'I wish you girls would get it together.' "

A major intent of the planning of LESFU was to document and develop the effectiveness of the new service delivery patterns, but the implementation of this desire was inadequate. The agency staff members gave only lip service to research; they were mainly skeptical and at times actually hostile toward it. Staff members were hired with no clear discussion of just what the research would require them to do. They were only told that there would be a research effort. Enmeshed in an admittedly difficult service job, the staff tended to view research as an unnecessary and unwanted burden.

The critical factor that strained the relationship between research and service was the complexity of the project itself. The staff was having trouble developing the methods of coordinating services that would be delivered, let alone establishing some sort of goal attainment scale. The complexity of mounting a sophisticated research effort along with a sophisticated service delivery had been greatly underestimated. Thus, early in the program a clear breakdown in communication between board and staff, between policy and implementation, occurred. This breakdown disrupted the agency. Staff members took their jobs on certain premises and came to resist any imposition or redirection of their work.

The board's subsequent discussions, which reaffirmed the importance of research, were specifically concerned with the issue of who should be eligible for the services of LESFU. It may be coincidental, but in the early summer of 1974, after a family social service bill was rejected in the state legislature, money seemed to be more available for sharply defined preventive work. Some board members of LESFU requested a meeting to discuss the policies and priorities of the union as a result of a summer progress report written by the chief consultant.

The informal meeting was well attended and the discussion animated. Earl Greenstreet, who perhaps knew the program more directly than any of the directors since the first team was housed at his settlement, expressed his concern openly about the nature of the program, the lack of specific selection criteria, and the possibility of the outreach system swamping the agency with more client needs than it could handle. Gold defended the broad focus and the concept of early prevention. She felt that, in order to achieve prevention, LESFU must work with all families in need of service; it would be short-sighted to work only with those in imminent danger of placement. The agency, understandably, wanted to establish itself in the community as offering needed services rather than having rigid eligibility requirements.

This meeting resulted in tightening up the approach, at least to the extent that some part of the team's efforts would be clearly directed toward narrowly defined prevention involving neglectful or abusive families at the door of Special Services for Children, families who ask to have their children placed, or families who have children in placement.

The board's discussion was clearly influenced by the need to "prove" that LESFU was accomplishing something, as well as by the genuine conviction that there were a great many multiproblem families, who needed special intensive efforts of the kind that the union could perhaps best arrange. But the need to show that something was actually happening at LESFU was also related to the increasing emphasis and interest that foundations and government agencies were placing on bottom-line figures. Research had to have high priority at LESFU.

In addition to revealing differences of opinion, the board meeting also showed a fundamental intellectual gap in LESFU's plan. Nowhere were the indexes of a family in imminent danger of having to place their children spelled out. In the words of one LESFU staff member, "How do we know who or what is a high-risk case?" Having never listed the dimensions of high risk, the staff understandably went to work with what ideas and concepts were available. If they came into contact with parents having trouble in family relationships or with their children, either in school or in the courts, then this was a family needing the service of LESFU. A project that is serious about research is one that has clearly spelled out indicators of its key concepts, especially those on which it will base its success or failure, prior to the beginning of its operations. Rue argued that this initial period during 1974 was actually a pretest, a time when, through staff experience, the actual indexes of high risk would be developed. What made this task more difficult was the fact that the staff had worked for many months without knowing that one of their tasks was to develop the index of high risk; this lack of information caused confusion and defiance.

The strain between research and service came to a head in the spring of 1975. At this point, state funding had been secured for the project; one aspect of this funding was the agreement by LESFU to research certain issues that the state was interested in for planning social services, such as the ability of LESFU to prevent unnecessary placement of children. The other research interest concerned the local impact of LESFU in preventing family break-up; this caused problems because the state insisted that LESFU restrict access to its services to people living in certain geographical areas, in this case, health areas according to census tracts.

This limitation created grave problems for the agency because staff members were not willing to deny service to people living one block outside the health area. They felt this would create a bad public image for a new agency. In addition, this restriction caused personal stress to staff members who had to refuse to help people outside of the area. After a series of negotiations, an agreement allowed LESFU to expand its boundaries to include those areas containing the majority of clients. Another state demand created more tension by insisting that LESFU specifically define the characteristics that would index high-risk families. The state researcher, David Livingston, was absolutely firm that without such an index it would be impossible to replicate LESFU's results. The discussions with Livingston dragged on throughout 1975.

The direction of the research effort of LESFU, from the state's point of view, was always related to larger issues of planning services, rather than to a specific concern about whether LESFU itself was a good project. Their emphasis was crucial; in April 1976, Livingston produced a document that had been awaited for several months. This document was supposed to state the design of a LESFU research effort, but it turned out to be a policy statement that had profound effects on LESFU.

In essence, the state said that it mattered little whether LESFU could prevent unnecessary placements or not, because previous studies have shown that the foster care system is in such chaos that families and children designated by the public welfare services as needing placement are not placed. Placement does not necessarily follow high risk. Whether unnecessary or not, most children are not placed because too many arbitrary factors intervene.

This report changed the rationale for LESFU. The central issue became the integration or development of a service system, rather than the prevention of unnecessary placement. Livingston suggested that he would like to research how and why the LESFU service model provided effective help for families. Thereafter, the essential focus of LESFU was the integration of services and the development of a case management mechanism. (How the agency responded to Livingston is noted in Chapter Five.)

Social history at LESFU was, like research, a strained relationship. There was one crucial difference: LESFU was funding the social history, so the funding source never influenced the social history as it did research. As noted earlier, Sarah Savant was originally hired as a social historian and then added the role of administrator. She noted that, from the beginning, the relationship of social history to the project was confused. On the grounds of confidentiality, as well as on the grounds that the staff would be reluctant to talk if a historian was present, the social historian and her assistant were excluded from some staff meetings at which they felt they should have been present.

In mid 1975 the board had a full discussion of the purpose of a social history with the team leaders present; the board wanted the social history to document the development of LESFU and to serve as an ongoing basis of feedback to appropriate staff members about key problems in the Family Union's operations. The discussion focused on the central issue of the historian's access to the program. The staff was adamant that they did not wish to be observed because this would inhibit service to clients, who would be reticent to speak and share intimate details of their lives—in essence, the program would be destroyed. But other factors were obviously at play besides sincere concern for clients. Some staff members were very anxious about being observed lest their inadequacies be exposed; others were concerned about loss of control and discretion over time and simply did not wish to be observed. Much of the discontent and anger over having to be observed was focused on the assistant historian, who was trained in anthropology, not social welfare. It was argued that she did not have the knowledge to make valid judgments about what they were doing, especially since she had very little experience in the community or knowledge of the local ethnic groups. The board decided that the social historian would have access to several clients from each team, so that she could develop a view of typical cases. This plan never worked well; the staff resisted by forgetting to tell the social historian about meetings, making the point that many clients did not speak English, and generally inviting the social historian only because the administration made it mandatory.

At the end of the first year of actual operation of LESFU, the social historian was observing worker-client interactions in a selected number of cases, was present at the development of contracts with agencies, and was monitoring the relationship of training to the actual implementation of the ideas discussed at the training sessions. Yet, it was clear that even as staff members became more cooperative, they were not convinced of the value of a social history. They were merely accommodating the historians and the wishes of the administration.

The board did not come to grips with the dilemmas and conflicts related to research and service and policy and implementation partly because their only real source of information about the program's operation was the staff. Also the board had to consider many other aspects of the program as important as research, such as developing contracts with the community and locating clients in need of service. Clearly, a board that is dependent on the staff for information about an agency's functioning is a board that will ultimately be controlled by the staff. A board cannot ask intelligent questions and be constructively critical if it does not have its own source of information. Additionally, before 1976, the board was mainly concerned with securing funds necessary to establish and begin the program.

This situation illustrates a basic administrative problem. Any agency has many tasks to perform. The question is, will the agency deal with these sequentially, will it attempt to do everything at once, or will it set definite priorities and consciously give priority to certain tasks? The LESFU experience shows that functions deemed vital to an organization tend to obscure the importance of other tasks. It was essential that LESFU deal with its funding problems, but it was also important for it to consider the options available for community representation, as well as the strains between equally valid goals of research and service.

If staff members tend to develop their jobs in terms of what they are most capable of doing, organizations will devote their resources first to what they are immediately constrained to do and second to what the staff is comfortable doing. This interest in immediate demands and lack of concern for the future causes problems. By January 1975, LESFU was in a state of crisis.

It was becoming clear to Rue and others that Savant and Gold had particular areas of expertise, but they could not work together. Savant's decision to leave in early 1975 presented the agency with an opportunity, which Rue was quick to seize. An advertisement was placed in various newspapers and résumés were received for the position of executive director. The final selection was made in front of the entire board. Four applicants sat around the table and the board sat in an outer circle. First, Rue asked a question and each of the applicants was given an opportunity to respond, then board members, if they so desired, asked questions. The only applicant to receive much support was Kenneth Brahms, who had a master's degree in business administration. After a few years in other fields, he had decided that social welfare was his main interest and he had worked for two social agencies, mainly in their fund-raising and business operation, although his last job had a measure of community organization related to it.

The sole substantive discussion by board members, after the interviews were concluded, related to the importance of an executive director being Chinese, Puerto Rican, or Black. The discussion was vague. No one made the point that this consideration is one of many variables and that the discussion should focus on what priority should be given to such variables.

Brahms was an attractive young man, obviously intelligent and sincere. As subsequent events will demonstrate, the choice of Brahms was a success. Once again the organization was helped immeasurably by its ability to change personnel; without such changes LESFU would not have recovered.

Nevertheless, the board did not realize the extent to which LESFU was in chaos at this time. One reason for this was the lack of any systematic accountability system. The board probably assumed that the agency was in a period of development and problems were to be expected. Yet, there were problems beyond those that one would expect. The board depended on the reports of either Savant or Gold; board meetings were always general, focused on the positive, and centered on current activities. Can a board, no matter how knowledgeable and expert, ensure accountability if it has no independent source of information? At this point in the agency's history the answer was certainly no. Without some control over sources of information, policy issues related to adjusting strains between means and ends will not surface at the board level. The search for alternative solutions to goal conflicts will be too quickly aborted and the tyrannies of time, money, and ideology unresisted.

With the hiring of Brahms on March 15, 1975, LESFU

began the systematic development of its service model. Exactly one year later the full complement of three teams was finally hired and working. The model of service, with its potentials and limitations, was coming to light. Problems notwithstanding, the agency had survived a turbulent period primarily because of the stability of its funding, the confidence of its board members in its service model, and the agency's ability to change personnel when the integrity of the model was threatened.

5

Engaging Troubled Families and Contracting for Services

After specifying goals, ideally, in developing a model, the first step is to separate all the component parts and arrange them in sequential or program order. Next comes a trial run in which gaps and unanticipated problems emerge. Brahms quickly found himself thrust into this process: "the model was rather clearly established, at least on paper, [but] it had not yet really been implemented. . . . The board can agree on things, but the staff has to implement them. And there were lots of questions that the staff had in relation to the value of those policies, in relation to the value of the contracts. 'You know, why have a contract? Why not just take people at their word, you can get more done that way . . . Trust is really the way to operate.' This was actually stated by team leaders and social work associates."

Fortunately for the agency, Brahms and Gold, after an

Note: This chapter draws substantially on field observations made by Elizabeth Howe.

55

initial testing period, developed a good working relationship and publicly supported each other. What disagreements they had were discussed privately. Gold was pleased to be relieved of administrative supervision and Brahms was happy with her training and competence in social work practices.

Local Workers

The difficulty in bringing order to the agency cannot be overestimated. A case in point is the structure and functioning of the teams. One of the requirements for hiring social work associates (SWAs) and homemakers (HMKs) was their residence or former residence in the immediate vicinity. It was hoped that a locally known staff would help the agency develop contracts. One lifetime resident and worker had a sister who worked in a settlement, a mother who worked in a local agency, and an uncle who owned the grocery store across the street; more relatives and friends lived near the agency. Furthermore, she had worked in local social work agencies and knew people in them and the agencies' capacities, red-tape requirements, and so on.

The principal strength to having local residents on staff was their ability to get immediate service for clients. They knew how to avoid bureaucratic delays and how to fulfill eligibility requirements of various public agencies. They could make other agencies accountable because friendship between the workers was a link beyond mutual concern for the client. Agencies knew about this reciprocity of service. Where LESFU could expect referrals and good service, these agencies expected their LESFU friends to help their clients when possible. Clients also felt freer to come for service than they did if the workers were unfamiliar. The city team (Team Three), whose workers were unknown to the area, received few walk-in clients during 1975 and 1976. Nevertheless, problems of a subtle nature emerged as a result of workers being local residents. Coming as a surprise to the administration, these problems probably could not have been anticipated:

1. *Outreach*. Most of the local agencies did not require outreach by their workers. Local workers' reputations were built on the

recommendations of satisfied clients who sent their friends to the same workers. SWAs found it demeaning to have to search for clients as outreach required.

2. *Contracts.* The idea of a written, signed agreement was highly objectionable to local agency workers, who believed *"la palabra es sagrado"*—the word is sacred. Again, reputations were built on word of mouth. SWAs were very reluctant to oppose this understanding; they did not want to alienate their friends working in the area, particularly because they were not certain that the contract system was a sounder service method.

3. *Monitoring.* Monitoring was particularly threatening to other agencies' workers. (See Chapter Seven for further discussion.) SWAs, in the 1975–1976 period, were reluctant to monitor contracts, again for fear of alienating friends as well as because they were unsure how to do it.

4. *Research.* For research purposes, two restrictions were placed on the team concerning the clients they could accept. No clients outside a set boundary and no clients not meeting the criterion of high risk of placement would be accepted for service. Not only was it emotionally difficult for workers to turn away their neighbors and friends, but other agencies were alarmed by social service workers turning away people in need. To balance these tensions, workers sometimes worked behind the lines helping nonclients as well as "legal" clients by taking both to the welfare office.

Toward a More Formal System

As long as an informal system varied among workers and teams, it posed a problem if the model was to be instituted. Gradually the power of the formal authority system increased. Initially, the mechanism used at LESFU to gain enthusiastic staff participation was maximal inclusion of the staff in decisions concerning the agency. Emphasis was placed upon the group, not the individual. As a group, the staff would decide the best method of running the agency, and as a group, they would do their best to implement the method. This system fostered adherance to some norms and made it less likely that the model would be developed as planned.

Chronologically, the shift away from the informal participation system occurred as follows:

- 1974 Fall

Team leader, two SWAs, one HMK (Team One members). Developing the methodology—constant changing borne only because the staff was fully involved in the process. The team leader had trouble exerting authority as line staff were full partners in suggesting changes.

- 1975 January

Second team added: one team leader, two SWAs, two HMKs. This team leader demanded complete authority—did not like the open decision process. The team leaders and Gold started to meet separately from line staff.

- 1975 Summer

The program was floundering; all concepts (high risk of placement, contracts, convened meeting, goal attainment scale, family union) needed tightening up. The tightening occurred by Brahms making specific demands on the team leaders for statistics spelling out accomplishments and his right to inspect any case folder and find every aspect of the case there, in order and up-to-date. Team leaders oversaw the cases more carefully and more frequently. Changes continued and training sessions remained a way of discovering the best way of doing something with everyone having equal voice. Team One leader fired.

- 1976 January

Leader of the third team hired. A full staff of thirty-two line staff was to be complete within two months. The third team leader, on loan from the city, had to be trained on LESFU history, purpose and procedures. The new leader came from a bureaucracy where right and wrong procedures were absolutes, and she demanded clarity in discussions. Team leader meetings with Brahms were regularized and line staff no longer had much part in decisions. Gold held regular meetings with the team leaders so training stopped being the locus of the decision-making process. Team leaders gave staff members an established policy or held meetings to hear their views, then passed these views back to Brahms or Gold. They asked Brahms for sanction to impose administrative order.

• 1976 March

The three teams' staffs complete. Training was divided into sections of team leaders, HMKs, and SWAs. Roles became distinguished as responsibilities were defined. The team leader now clearly coordinated the team by knowing the responsibilities of the team as a whole and of the SWAs and the HMKs separately. SWAs were forced to rely on the team leader rather than upon each other for help in their cases, for securing new families for service, and for getting HMK help. Brahms announced that either the SWAs develop family service contracts or leave. The contracts were the core of the methodology demonstrated by LESFU. By being so revolutionary, the contracts threatened the team staff. The SWAs were willing to use this new method only if they were guaranteed full team leader support. To meet Brahms' ultimatum they were forced to rely on their team leaders. SWAs had the burden and responsibility of being the agency's key service deliverers—the case managers. The importance attributed to this role by Brahms and Gold—a rise in status—lessened the impact of their loss of decision-making power in the agency.

This process of increasing team leader authority and reducing open forums for decisions was slow and subtle. The SWAs only recognized the changes retrospectively.

Team Integration

The informal system was further disrupted in the fall of 1975, when Brahms decided that the teams would be more effective if they were ethnically mixed. At that time, the Hispanic team had mainly Spanish-speaking clients and the Oriental team mainly Chinese clients.

Initially, the team leaders did not wish to change, but there was little opposition, because Sunnie Gold did not strongly oppose the change and the city team was racially mixed. Brahms felt that it would be difficult for the agency to operate with both integrated and segregated teams. He also felt that integration per se was valuable: "If your entire team is Hispanic, and your entire other team is Chinese, it sets up, one, an overly competitive situation along ethnic lines, and secondly . . . a breeding ground for the kind of prejudices that lie in almost all people who are proud of their own group and suspicious of other ethnic groups. And it exists on the Lower East Side as well as anywhere." By integrating the teams, Brahms hoped to avoid reinforcing such prejudices, if not eliminate them.

Integration was accomplished by adding new staff members to both teams, rather than by trading or firing staff members. Unintentionally, this shift further disrupted the informal system that had developed. Within the teams, the new workers—the black worker on the Spanish team, for example—were quick to speak up informally in the office, in team meetings, or to the team leader when they felt cultural behaviorisms were being given unnecessary emphasis, or if the workers were unconsciously alienating black clients by continuing to speak Spanish and offering only Spanish refreshments.

Integration also made a significant difference in the communication and cooperation among the teams. The Chinese member of the Spanish team would visit the Chinese team, often bringing a fellow (Spanish) team member. The Spanish worker in the Chinese team might see things differently than her Chinese teammates and felt free to say so at training sessions because there were other Hispanics who would recognize her viewpoint. This cross identification by the team members may have provided the fundamental insurance of open communication between the teams. The we-versus-they discussions were dispelled. The barriers of physical distance, language differences, and noncoordination in outreach and case activities did not alienate the teams.

Supervision

Further integration might have helped SWAs maintain a perspective of the agency's methodology in the face of familiar cultural patterns, which seemed unchangeable. The most important factor that kept the SWAs and HMKs oriented toward the service model and supportive of the emerging formal authority system was the weekly training session led by Sunnie Gold. Expressing confidence in the agency, she was a role model with whom many could identify personally even if they were dubious about contracting, monitoring, and the like. As a result of weekly training sessions, a degree of order was introduced into the work at LESFU. Team leaders—the actual supervisors of the workers—were present at all training sessions, enabling them, along with Gold, to clarify problems of practice. In their day-by-day work, the leaders attempted to ensure that workers were following the methods and techniques discussed in training sessions.

Supervision of individual workers was also a primary factor in maintaining the formal authority system. Although a bachelor's degree was not a requirement for the social work associate job and a high school diploma was not necessary for the homemaker, the more sophisticated workers, verbally and in writing, worked at an accelerated pace in comparison to the less articulate workers during the 1975–1976 period. The discrepancy was gradually revealed in their ability to see families' problems as a whole, to maneuver local and public agency workers to help clients, and to write records in a concise manner. The less-skilled workers received intensive help during supervision in which training sessions were reexplained and reemphasized.

Most staff members enjoyed training because it gave them

the material and the power to make individual, responsible decisions. The respect for their own judgment made them more perceptive. The intellectual complexity of their job at LESFU distinguished them from other social service workers in the area. Some individual workers accomplished a great deal. The following case provides an example; a custodian of a neighborhood tenement reported that one of the tenants spent nearly all her days crying locked in her apartment. LESFU immediately scheduled a few home visits by a SWA who reported the following situation:

> The client is a Vietnam refugee with four children aged six to fourteen years. She lost her husband and her youngest son in Vietnam. She has no relatives or friends in this country and does not speak English. (The social work associate communicates with her in Cantonese.) Her small apartment was completely bare except for two beds. The small allotment received from public assistance was not sufficient to buy furniture or clothing and no special allowance had been provided for these purposes. The situation was potentially serious—all the family possessed was warm-weather clothing and winter was approaching.
>
> The children, because of their home situation and inability to communicate, had problems in school. The fact that the family had been affluent in Vietnam compounded the difficulties they were experiencing, and the mother felt that she might be on the verge of a breakdown.
>
> The LESFU social work associate worked with the client to determine the family's service needs. They identified five major areas including:
>
> 1. Financial—more money required for family's basic needs.
> 2. Socialization—human contact needed particularly by mother.
> 3. Language—need by all family members to learn English.
> 4. Health—children's teeth particularly in need of work.
> 5. Housing—need for larger apartment.
>
> A meeting was scheduled with potential service providers and a service plan was formulated. The LESFU staff monitored the provision of services and the participation of the client. The following services have been provided to the family:

1. After considerable negotiation, the International Rescue Committee supplied $600 for furniture, $275 for winter clothing and $80 for a sewing machine.

2. A neighbor agreed to help the mother shop and along with the LESFU worker (who initially visited the woman four times a week), provided some of the human contact that was needed.

3. The mother and children were enrolled in special English classes provided by the Board of Education and Immigration Social Services. The immigration service, which ordinarily charges a fee, agreed to waive it.

4. Gouverneur Hospital gave all members of the family physical check-ups and provided the dental work required by the children (root-canal work and teeth extraction).

5. A local agency, It's Time, contracted to work with the family in finding more appropriate housing.

6. Client participation:

Since the mother still had considerable time on her hands, especially when the children were in school, and since she was still hard pressed to make ends meet, she agreed to seek employment. The mother knew of an opening for an assistant clerk at the grocery store where she bought her food each day but had been afraid to ask for the job since she had never worked in Vietnam. The LESFU worker helped her ask for the job and spoke to the store owner about the family's situation. The store owner hired the client. The mother is pleased with the job. Besides providing additional revenue, she has been able to meet a number of new people through her work. The family is now able to cope better with their situation. The LESFU worker currently meets with the family once a week to check on how things are progressing, to assess any new developments and to help the family begin to do some longer-range planning. As an additional precaution, since a new crisis could erupt anytime for the family, LESFU has arranged to make emergency help available to this woman and her family twenty-four hours a day.

Without assistance, it is conceivable that within a short time the four children would have wound up in foster care. Communication was a major impediment to developing a successful working relationship with the client. In providing services to the family, the LESFU staff was able to coordinate:

1. Public Agency Services (Board of Education, Immigration)
2. Voluntary Agency Service (It's Time)
3. Charitable Organization (International Rescue)
4. Neighborhood Supports (Neighbor assists with shopping)
5. Overall Management Supports (LESFU)

Through LESFU services, this family was kept intact and has now been informed that the husband and son who had been assumed dead in Vietnam have been located and will be joining the family in New York.

Training

Notwithstanding the excellent work by staff members, the agency relied too heavily on training. If the only problem in the agency had been the adequacy of the skills, values, and capacities of individual workers, training might have been sufficient. But the agency was beset by more serious problems. Much of what it hoped to achieve was related to factors outside its immediate control—that is, the willingness of other agencies to cooperate—and the necessity to adapt the service model to fit unanticipated contingencies. A very sophisticated staff could probably have adapted the model as they were trained. (The original plan for training led to the chaotic situation noted in the preceding chapter.) The LESFU staff members varied greatly in sophistication and capacity, and the shift from the informal to a more formal authority base did not lessen anxiety. Staff members could no longer go around the mine field; they had to use the service model, whether it blew up in their faces or not. In such a situation, it is not surprising that adaptations developed.

Outreach. To help families struggling with an extreme situation, the teams first had to find and identify the families. These are families that often do not acknowledge or realize that they need help or know how to seek assistance. Many have previously sought help and not received it and have given up trying.

Originally, staff members were trained to understand that parents in these families rarely, if ever, leave their apartments and do not let their children go out. They are not known or are forgotten by other agencies; the only way they can be found is by knocking on their door. Door-to-door outreach was difficult. Team staffs were afraid to go door-to-door in unlocked, dark buildings and people frequently did not open their doors to strangers. Enough severe cases were being referred to build legitimate caseloads without seeking these families.

The concept of finding families not seen by anyone and barely surviving was gradually dropped. Instead, the families served were known by many agencies but perennially lost, since they needed more service than individual agencies were equipped to give. By early 1975, it was recognized that the target population would largely include families known to local agencies.

Perhaps what was most unanticipated was the frustration the teams had in dealing with families with high risk of placement. After they were located, some of these families were the most resistant to coming to meetings, developing a contract, and using the goal attainment scale. The years of neglect, frustration, and struggling were not going to be erased simply because a social worker was at the door and was interested in giving help.

Engagement. The workers' frustration was mainly felt at the second step in LESFU's service delivery model, engagement. The initial interview, the first step in the engagement process, determined whether a person had a high risk of placement. Within one month of contact or in three visits or less, a fact sheet was filled out with the vital information about the client and a summary of the client's interviews was written that assessed high risk, the problems that needed work, and a plan for attacking the problems. A goal attainment scale was written for each problem area, in an attempt to set possible goals: the best possible outcome, a satisfactory outcome, a less-than-satisfactory outcome, the worst possible outcome. For example, with a truant child, the best possible outcome would be if the child returned to school and showed new interest in learning. An acceptable outcome would be a return to school and an end of truancy, a less-than-favorable outcome would be occasional truancy, and the worst possible outcome would be no change at all.

In developing the goal attainment scale with a client, a work agreement is made: the worker and the client agree to do certain things, ideally. Yet, the workers were tremendously frustrated with this process because of additional problems with the clients. First, clients' emergencies, such as the theft of a welfare check or the disappearance of a child or husband, often took precedence over their goals. Second, clients seldom understood the value of the goal attainment scale and were often not interested in meeting to discuss it; workers constantly had to chase the clients. Third, after the emergency was met, many clients were not interested in service, such as that supplied by a homemaker.

In most cases during 1975 and 1976, the goal attainment scales were written after the fact in order to satisfy the requirements of the administration, thereby having little impact on clients. One obstacle was the fear of the social work associates and, to a certain extent, the team leaders that they were being set up for negative evaluations, simply because progress with clients was not as linear and straightforward as the goal attainment scales implied.

Nevertheless, engagement is the most crucial aspect of the LESFU model. If clients are unmotivated to participate or feel that they cannot be helped, the most effective arrangement and array of services cannot help. How to engage the client was the most difficult task for staff members to learn. Social work lacks a theory of engagement that can easily be taught. Also, the formal, written work agreements and family service contracts could be developed by dint of the workers' energy. (Brahms had in fact told the SWAs "either do the contracts or ship out.") The pressure to write contracts during 1975 and 1976 worked against the necessity to engage clients, In some cases, contracts were written before clients were fully engaged or willing to consistently work on their problems. Premature contracts were not beneficial. To engage a client properly required an intense investment of energy, patience, faith, and knowledge of when to listen, wait, act, encourage, and confront. This process took time; it did not occur at an intake or initial interview.

Perhaps the most potent engagement factor that the workers had to overcome was emotional fatigue. There was more security in doing all the work by themselves than in prodding and encouraging the client to take responsibility. The workers could invest their time and energy and feel personal gratification with the results without dealing with the confusion of the client's emotions. In some ways, the structure of the contract provided a sense of support in comparison to the amorphous nature of engagement, but it presented other problems.

The Family Service Contract

In social work, the *contract* has generally been defined as an agreement between client and worker that sets forth the purpose of their interaction and the ways to achieve that purpose (Malluccio and Marlow, 1974). The contract is intended to start breaking the dependency cycle of clients by clearly spelling out the tasks that they could do on their own. By also defining the workers' obligations, a clear contractual exchange is set up, rather than having the workers do everything.

There are three components to developing the family service contract: (1) meeting with all servicing agents who will be helping the client; (2) writing the contract and getting it signed; (3) overseeing the resulting service. Each of these components was abrasively new to all the local agency workers. Many agencies claimed they followed this process but not in such a degradingly formal fashion. The LESFU workers had two hurdles: to understand the procedure fully and to overcome other agency workers' resistance.

Convening the Meetings. Most workers were reluctant to call the involved workers of other agencies to a formal meeting. They did not have master's degrees in social work, often did not speak fluent English, and were usually younger than the local professionally trained social workers. To call these agencies and ask that the involved worker attend a meeting was extremely threatening to the SWAs.

The SWAs understood the value of getting the workers together with the client—decisions are made simultaneously, necessary information is given openly, and commitments made publicly. However, this value did not outbalance the fear of being verbally abused by requesting a meeting and, further, of being inarticulate at the meeting.

For the initial convened meetings, the team leaders helped the social work associates by role playing, discussing possible problems, and attending the meetings themselves. The workers were forced to hold the meetings but were supported in their effort. Everyone on a team knew when a SWA was holding a meeting, especially if it was to handle a particularly difficult problem. All of the team supported the SWA with encouragement and such last-minute details as getting coffee and arranging chairs. Afterward, the SWA discussed the meeting with the team leader and usually with his or her team members.

Public speaking, not an easily learned skill, is not usually required for nonprofessionals in the field. The workers had to learn a special type of self-assurance to conduct these meetings. All participants had to be encouraged to contribute, commitments had to be exacted, and the client's reaction had to be stated publicly. In addition, convening meetings between service providers and clients was an uncharted area. Inevitably, errors were made as the techniques of convening were developed. Given the complexity of the task, it is surprising that the relatively unskilled staff persevered.

Initially, too much emphasis was placed on meeting the requirements of convening the agents. Some meaningless meetings were held; when a meeting was unnecessary for an agreement, because services had already been arranged, the meeting was held before the client was ready. The service then failed due to a lack of client cooperation. Sometimes more information came out in the meeting than could be dealt with, such as unknown marital conflict or competition between two workers from different agencies. The most disorganized clients—the target population—took far longer than two months to be emotionally and intellectually ready to participate responsibly in the meetings. With some clients, the two month requirement set by Brahms and Gold between the first interview and the first contract meeting took priority over a more prolonged attempt to prepare the client.

There were a number of other complicating factors. Staff members of other agencies did not understand the use of the contract. Many of the services they gave were needed by LESFU clients on an emergency basis, and they did not see the purpose of writing the contract, for the sake of monitoring, after providing help. Other agencies felt that they already provided many services for the family, and they considered the contract system an additional and unnecessary burden. There was also the question of agency priorities. These were busy people who felt they did not have time to attend meetings about an abstract concept. They also wanted to avoid control of their priorities by another organization.

Writing the Contract. The contract was actually the formal minutes of the meeting, written and typed afterward and sent to the participants for signed confirmation of the agreements. The workers had two problems with this procedure. First, they frequently lacked experience with formal writing and could not write fluently in English; they had great difficulty writing clearly and concisely. Most SWAs felt vulnerable making their composition public; they frequently procrastinated and worried over this task. Second, the SWAs feared being insulted if they demanded a signature. To sidestep this problem, they were encouraged to write a rough draft at the meeting and to ask for the signatures then.

Monitoring the Contract. Monitoring was unanimously misunderstood by other agencies. By acting as the contract coordinator, the LESFU worker had the right to oversee the services, see that deadlines were met, inform the agent if the client seemed legitimately dissatisfied, and keep communication open among all involved agencies. The SWAs were given training on monitoring diplomatically. Nevertheless, a question remained, what is overseeing and what is evaluating service? The latter was not within the monitoring role, yet, problems arose from inadequate service, rather than missed deadlines or a lack of communication.

For most contracts, the SWAs succeeded in getting an agreement and satisfactory service, but these agreements were often related to specific tasks, such as daycare, transportation, and tutoring. The problems occurred in contracts for more general services— guidance counseling in school, psychiatric counseling, medical examination, and legal advising.

There was little systematic monitoring during 1975 and 1976. Many of the contracts were too general; the specific tasks to be monitored were not clear. SWAs felt they were in the position of supplicants needing the cooperation of other workers and they feared alienating them. As cases were explored, there were additional needs for more service and SWAs were frequently calling workers for additional help.

Closing the Case. The teams also had problems with closing cases. When is a high-risk, extremely chaotic family brought to stability? How can this point be recognized? Besides this conceptual problem, the work entailed in engaging a new client was so great that workers were reluctant to close a case. There were several reasons for this. In two years, the teams still had not attained the fifteen high risk cases per worker quota. To make the caseloads larger they prolonged closing a case. Workers also grew attached to the families. On a less positive side, if family situations crumbled immediately after SWAs ended their involvement, it might be revealed that they had not properly engaged the client at the commencement of service—the client had only followed the worker without developing new understanding and strength.

Clearly, the development of the service model was not easy. John Goya, the team leader of the predominantly Puerto Rican team, summarized the challenge: "The staff is caught trying to fit the concept to the people and their problems. If not done with skill, the result can be weak contracts with high-risk families or nonhigh-risk families with strong contracts."

Team Leaders Versus the Board

The frustration over the contracts came out in the team leaders' relationship to the board. The leaders could not understand why the local agencies were not more anxious to cooperate, since the executives of these agencies were all on LESFU's board.

At the March 1976 board meeting, Frank Mode of Jefferson House, a settlement, said that his staff was concerned about LESFU and confused about its purpose and function. In particular, they questioned the agency contract and its implementation. Harvey Cardinal, the Monroe House director, noted that some of this misunderstanding was a result of the directors' agreeing to the agency contracts without consulting their staffs. Judge Berk, a director of another large settlement, said that he thought the word *monitoring* was a problem; some staff members felt they were being controlled. He suggested that *follow-up* might be a better word.

Earl Greenstreet said that the problems at his settlement were being resolved case by case. He suggested that the directors look at the nature of LESFU contracts with their staff and report the results at the next board meeting. The LESFU staff would also present their own view of why they were having trouble developing contracts with agencies.

All of these questions came up even though Brahms had put a great deal of effort and time into developing the agency contracts, as the following example demonstrates:

> In order to provide comprehensive services for children and families of the Lower East Side of Manhattan, the Harold Street Settlement agrees to enter into a contractual arrangement with the Lower East Side Family Union, a community-based child welfare agency, effective on June 1, 1975 to be periodically reviewed at the request of either the settlement or the union.
>
> The purpose of this agreement is to develop higher quality integrated services for community families, and, by working together with these families, to strengthen the quality of child and family life in the community.
>
> To realize the common goal of supporting existing families' structures, the settlement and the Family Union agree to the following forms of cooperation, which draw upon the unique strengths of each individual agency:
>
> 1. It is agreed that individual service contracts will be written by the Lower East Side Family Union and Harold Street Settlement for each family selected for services.
>
> It is agreed that families to be considered for contractual agreements between the Lower East Side Family Union and Harold Street Settlement will have a high risk of placement of one or more children and will be characterized by a highly uncertain quality of family life. Some examples of the families which might be selected are those with one or more of the following characteristics:
>
> a. Have already indicated a desire to place their child.
>
> b. Have a child who has formerly been in placement.
>
> c. Have a child already living outside the home, either through formal placement or other informal arrangement.
>
> d. There is a mother with severe medical or psychiatric problems, and there is indication that the child is having problems in normal development.
>
> e. There is a child with severe psychiatric or physical impairment with which the family has been unable to cope.

f. The parents are physically separated but no legal determination has been made.

g. A child in the family has lived with different family members over the years.

h. Child abuse or maltreatment is suspected.

This list is neither inclusive nor exclusive. Families with none of the characteristics listed but experiencing other problems may be selected. Each case will be separately judged and selection for service will be based on mutual acceptance by Harold Street Settlement and the Lower East Side Family Union.

2. For each of these families it is agreed that individual service contracts will be written by the Family Union and Harold Street Settlement allowing those families to participate in Settlement programs within the guidelines and statutory regulations of the individual programs (for example, fee schedule established for daycare).

The Lower East Side Family Union will have responsibility for initiating steps to develop the individual contracts and for monitoring the contracts. Monitoring will involve taking all necessary steps to ensure that the plan agreed upon is carried out by all parties to the contract and will include periodically reconvening the parties to discuss progress made and new developments.

From time to time it will become necessary to modify or prematurely terminate a service plan. This shall only be done for compelling reasons and with the acquiescence of the monitoring agency.

Monitoring shall not include authority over the quality of work provided by Harold Street Settlement staff, assuming they are meeting the requirements of the contract.

Within the limitations of staffing, funding, research, and agency policy, Harold Street Settlement and the Lower East Side Family Union agree that referrals made by either agency to the other will be given high priority for participation in their respective programs.

3. The Lower East Side Family Union and Harold Street Settlement staffs will develop jointly and participate in training sessions based on needs identified by the Family Union.

4. The Family Union will make provisions for the exchange of relevant information and referrals through conferences and other agreed upon means.

5. The Family Union will provide information and education about the union's activities and resources to persons involved in the settlement's programs. The settlement will aid the Family Union in identifying and reaching potential members as well as to help the union increase its membership.

6. The Family Union and Harold Street Settlement shall, from time to time, share in agency planning procedures in order to provide for more cost-effective services and prevention of duplicate overhead costs.

7. The Harold Street Settlement will assist the Family Union in its fund-raising activities and grant applications but will bear no responsibility or liabilities for the expenditure of funds.

8. The Family Union will assist the settlement in making recommendations for new programs and expanded areas of services to families in the community. The Family Union will also take a leadership role in suggesting public policy issues on which the settlement and the union may want to take further action.

9. Harold Street Settlement staff will cooperate with efforts to develop a social history of the Lower East Side Family Union through discussions, meetings, and sharing of information with social history staff.

_____   _____
Executive Director   Executive Director
Harold Street Settlement   Lower East Side Family Union

The board discussion about contracting was quite animated and implied some criticism of the staff. Henry Rue made the point that simply because the executives had discussed the LESFU programs with their staffs did not mean necessarily that the staffs agreed or were willing to cooperate. The team leaders considered the main problem a lack of communication by the directors, who had not exerted all of their influence. Rue tried repeatedly to explain that directors have trouble continually monitoring the actions of their staffs and that their power is considerably less than expected.

The contracting and agency cooperation issue was given only superficial treatment at the April 1976 board meeting. Mode, who had initiated the discussion at the past meeting, was absent. The board was mainly concerned with the point raised by the state research consultant that the state was no longer interested in demonstration projects related to preventing placement. The state felt that existing evidence showed that placement could be avoided if services were available and that it was impossible to carry out a scientific study at LESFU since high risk could not be defined. LESFU had to reconsider its main focus.

None of the directors had discussed the issue of their relationship to LESFU with their staff, so they had nothing to report. The LESFU staff was not asked to present its point of view even though it had discussed the issue; it was deferred to a later meeting. This postponement had unfortunate consequences; team leaders privately were angry. They felt that the board set policies without concerning itself with implementation. Instead of being actively involved in promoting cooperation, the board, according to the staff, was passive in developing cooperation. Staff members began to question the legitimacy of the board.

The relationship between the board and the team leaders, which had never been good, grew severely strained. The board seemed unaware of its implied criticism of the staff at the March meeting and, although there were more immediate issues to discuss, missed the importance of this discussion to the staff. In turn, the staff failed to communicate the necessity of this discussion to the board.

From the outset of the organization, staff participation at board meetings was difficult. Most of the board executives ran boards in their own agencies without staff presence on a regular basis. The board of LESFU did not realize the difference it would make to have staff members present at every board meeting. They had not wondered if people working intimately and full-time with problems could sit back and let them make policies affecting these problems, especially when staff members think these policies are based on limited information. In addition, the team leaders were rather young and had little experience in dealing with a board. They possessed a limited concept of board and administrative functions. The situation was ripe for misunderstanding.

At the April 1976 board meeting, the main concern was the new focus of the state research effort, involving research and demonstration in the area of integrating services. The contract system that

LESFU had developed was particularly interesting to the state. From the board's perspective, the discussion about relationships among the agencies would no doubt reoccur; they felt no need to discuss it immediately.

The team leaders had been forced into the classic foreman role—the person in the middle. They were under pressure from Brahms and the board above and from the staff below. The board became a focus for their frustration. Brahms, an obviously competent, hard-working person who tried to help them with their real responsibility difficulties, was not an inviting target, since he appreciated their efforts. In formalizing the agency, the increase in hostility and frustration was an unanticipated consequence; there was no plan for dealing with it, but it had unfortunate side effects.

The agency's effort to establish the Family Union was a case in point. A community organizer, hired to implement community development projects to promote a family union—an idea presented in the consultant's report initially received little cooperation from the team leaders, who were struggling, along with the SWAs, to operationalize the service model. Staff members, including Brahms, were unclear about what the community organizer would do. The consultant's proposal seemed general and the board had no clear concept of what they wanted the organizer to achieve and how. This vagueness inevitably taxed the staff, according to the team leaders.

The community organizer was hired with the clear understanding that he would use the team leaders' time as little as possible, a point emphasized during the hiring interview. When the community organizer joined the staff, the team leaders made certain he attended their meetings with Brahms and board meetings, but they were equally insistent about not permitting him to speak to the SWAs without first clearing it with them and not actively volunteering suggestions when he requested them. Community organization had become one of many irritations.

At the May board meeting, Brahms attempted to alert the board to the staff's frustration by reporting the obstacles the staff had been facing: "The high-risk family is often unable to meet contract commitments. They have to be almost dragged to appointments and meetings. While our motto is supposed to be short-term service, high-risk families may require years of support and in some cases might need support until the children are old enough to lead independent lives."

The team leaders considered the discussion inconclusive. They wanted concrete statements of policy, but the board discussed the problems generally. Rue said, as Brahms had, that some families need prolonged, sustained help. There was some discussion of developing peer supports in the neighborhood, as has been done in other countries. Rue said that there was a possibility, given an additional $25 thousand from a local foundation, to begin to work in an adjacent area. Perhaps in this area LESFU might develop the self-help model, which could be more appropriate to long-term care cases. He then initiated the discussion of the new directions that LESFU must take if it was to become a permanent organization. This discussion was the high point of the team leaders' frustration with the board. They wanted some indication from the board of appreciation for the difficulty they were having carrying out the agency's policies and some reconsideration of what exactly they were expected to do.

As noted earlier, the ramifications of having team leaders attend board meetings were not completely understood when this policy was initiated. Probably the key difference between a board meeting where staff regularly attend and where they do not lies in the staff's greater sensitivity to criticism when present at meetings. Implied criticism and an apparent lack of appreciation for achievements were negative side effects of the team leaders' attendance.

However, the board was undoubtedly correct in focusing on the problems of a more permanent source of funding for the agency. Early action in considering how to institutionalize a demonstration project is essential, or the possibility of permanence may be lost. Decisions on institutionalizing a program are not simply rational or based on merit; they are also political. And the more complex the politics of permanence, the more time and energy must go into dealing with permanency.

Rue introduced the question of permanence in a straightforward manner:

> The big question in making anything permanent
> today is that there is no new money to make anything.

Therefore, I think that our posture should no longer be that we can demonstrate that we can prevent foster care. We are demonstrating how to integrate services in a district in a way that will make it less likely that youngsters will go into foster care. . . . The LESFU-like structure is not only good for preventing foster care, it is good for preventing a lot of disabilities. And it is not [just] for families in relation to foster care or alcoholism or child neglect or delinquency.

Charter revision . . . probably will result in a redefinition of the community planning district. It will also give the Community Planning Board substantial new powers. Again, no one is quite sure how extensive, but it is assumed that they will have considerable impact. And they are to know something that is not now known: how much money comes into a district, for what purposes, and how it is spent on whom. . . . Special Services for Children is required under the new charter revisions to be coterminous with the community planning districts. It is one of the few social service agencies of the city that is required to meet the coterminality mandate for charter revision. There is a definite service planning function in the new planning boards. One idea we might follow is to get foundations interested in helping the community planning board move towards developing LESFU-like structures.

When Rue asked for comments to his proposal, there was little discussion. Most of the board members had not realized what they were to hear at this meeting, although Rue's comments should not have come as a surprise to anyone who knew the history of LESFU.

The episode at this board meeting was in many ways symbolic of the way LESFU was created. Broad concepts were presented; they were substantive and rational but they were not operational. As support and fund-raising devices, the concepts were excellent, but they needed to be operationalized for the program. Additionally, staff members had a limited picture of the development of LESFU, the early concerns for service integration, and how the project developed. They were concerned about doing their job and having some recognition and help.

The staff was very much in the rational tradition—prove something, then make it permanent. Rue came out of a different tradition. Social problems are seldom completely solved; they are redefined as the limitations and potentials of problems, conceptions, and solutions are understood. Thus, the problem of unnecessary placement was not really solved; it was redefined by LESFU (Rittel and Webber, 1977)', then redefined again.

Summary

From a program planning point of view, it is doubtful if anyone could have predicted the specific internal problems and dysfunctions that resulted from the ethnicity and local residence of social work associates, the frustrations that would result from operationalizing the model, the board versus staff tension, or the goal displacement that resulted from the necessary formalization of the authority system. Yet, it is clear that in designing a program, mechanisms for program audits must be set up to reveal such issues. Simply assuming that executives can expose unanticipated problems by virtue of their position will not suffice.

Even without these audits, LESFU was able to move forward in developing its service model, albeit with considerable strain during 1975 and 1976. Brahms' following comments clarify a major reason why the organization was able to build a firm foundation that led to its continuous growth.

> During a period when trial and error must take place, adaptations and clarifications can lead to controversy and potential for undermining. You *must* have a strong, capable and committed middle-management group to pull through this period. We have had that and the team leaders deserve credit for the progress we have been able to make. They have been of immeasurable help on administrative and policy matters. They recognized the need for unity with administration. *They* were the ones who took the model and made the necessary adaptations to make it functional. They were the ones who had to answer the questions: What should a Family Service

Contract look like? How do you convene a meeting of providers with clients so that you get positive results? How do you get social workers and homemakers to function as a team? How do you motivate staff? and dozens more. A remarkable effort, I think.

Unity between the executive and the middle managers, provided they possess other requisite administrative and technical skills, is probably the crucial factor for success or failure during a project's implementation phase. At LESFU, the board's commitment, flexibility, and intelligence were important factors for success.

In the spring of 1976, when the state insisted that placement could not be predicted because the high-risk factors did not predict actual placements, the board kept its focus on the same families the agency had been working with but removed the predictive element from the definition of high risk. The accepted definition became families with characteristics comparable to families that have been sending their children into placement. This redefinition kept LESFU in the mainstream of government funding and service concerns without sacrificing the essence of the agency. Rue's further shift from simply preventing family break-up to averting a variety of other disruptions moved the agency toward concentration on developing its technique of service integration, even though the clients remained families with serious child-related problems. LESFU would have to refine its techniques before it could understand its effects on any social problem.

6

Using
Organizational Tension
to Improve Service
to Families

The turning points in the development of an organization are a type of history. By September 1976, LESFU had arrived at a significant turn: Title IV–B research and development funds were no longer available.

A proposal had been written to secure funding under the New York State Department of Social Services special funding for preventive services, such as foster care, for the 1976–1977 program year. The essential difference between prevention funds and the former Title IV–B funds was that prevention required dollar-for-dollar matching and Title IV–B did not. LESFU was fortunate that it had foundation grants to cover the match. But it was clear to the board and Brahms that this funding source might not suffice past September 1977 because the commitments from most of the foundations were due to expire during 1977.

By this point in the agency's history a strong management

team was in place. Brahms had grasped the essential details of his job and was now able to turn his attention to some of the organization's basic structural problems.

Many of the developmental problems of LESFU were the result of an original design error: the job requirements for social work associates were too difficult; probably the most skilled of workers would have had trouble carrying them out. Formal responsibilities of SWAs included: (1) outreach; (2) crisis assistance; (3) early assessment of high risk; (4) identification of special services needed; (5) work agreement with client (the goal attainment scale); (6) meeting with all provider agencies; (7) development and writing of the family service contract; (8) monitoring the contracts; and (9) follow-up and evaluation of the effectiveness of services as outlined in the family service contract. In addition to those activities, the social work associate must participate in team meetings, weekly training sessions, and weekly supervisory meetings with the team leader. SWAs' paperwork included monthly statistics, an intake sheet, a face (fact) sheet, monthly summaries, contracts, records of contracts, and termination, all for each case.

The administration failed to recognize that the social work associate job became increasingly complex as time progressed. The SWAs began by doing traditional neighborhood service work, advocating for clients with various public departments, and making referrals for needed service. Then outreach was introduced to find the most disintegrated families. Next, they had to assess the probability of placement, determine goal attainment scales, and finally develop the methodology of writing contracts and how to monitor them.

An added complication was the very nature of the work. Working with the most crisis-ridden families is not the same as screening families for adoption or handling teen club groups in a settlement house. The agency's administration had to deal with the stress and strain on workers. The following case illustrates this point:

A family of five children and a mother was referred to LESFU from a contract agency (Gouverneur Hospital), which was having difficulty getting follow-up on a medical examination. The mother had begun but dropped out of a comprehensive medical examination series at Gouverneur Hospital; she

was suspected of having cancer of the cervix and the youngest of
the five children had a heart condition. The family lived in a
one-bedroom tenement. Two of the children, of school age, had
never even been registered for school. Only three of the children were on the family's public assistance budget. Their diet
was almost exclusively starch and major nutritional deficiencies
were surfacing.

The LESFU staff began working with the family to
develop a service contract. Simultaneously, provider agencies
were contacted and a plan was developed. The LESFU staff
began to work with the mother in addressing school-related
problems and her need to deal with her medical problems as
soon as possible. Through a coordinated services approach
monitored closely by the LESFU workers, the following resulted:

> A worker from Gouverneur Hospital arranged appointments
> for needed family health services while the LESFU social
> worker convinced the mother to continue her hospital tests.
> The mother did have cancer, which was successfully removed.
> The LESFU social worker helped register the children for
> school and provided a homemaker assistant to get the chil-
> dren off to school. The homemaker also worked with the
> mother in the need for and preparation of nutritious, balanced
> meals at low cost. A recalculation of the family's public
> assistance grant for the addition of the two children that had
> been omitted was arranged with the Department of Social
> Services (DSS).
> A worker from a neighborhood agency, It's Time, began
> helping the family find larger living quarters.
> A worker from Special Services for Children of DSS pro-
> vided counseling on child-rearing responsibilities to the
> mother.

A variety of agency services was integrated into a service plan,
monitored by LESFU and delivered with the client's participation. Had the cancer gone untreated, there would have been an
additional five foster care cases, not to mention the human cost
of children receiving absolutely no education and losing their
mother.

As John Goya said, "It's hard to realize the stress these cases
put on workers. It is really a little overwhelming to keep all the

pieces together." Yet the year of June 1976 to June 1977 was relatively stable and productive for a variety of reasons: ease of adaptability related to the small size of the agency, unanticipated latent functions of procedures that maintained agency morale, the hard work of the staff, and Brahms' supportive, active leadership.

Training

Without regular, weekly training, the organization could have collapsed. Nevertheless, the social work associate job was so complex that the agency needed to consider different ways of breaking and combining tasks to achieve its ends. The issue that should have been debated was, do we need more training or do we need a new structure? Yet, without training, the service model could never have started. In addition, the anxiety that workers felt was channeled by the training sessions, which helped reduce tension. The more verbal workers raised problems with the service model, and training legitimized the workers' right to question what was happening.

Training also was occasionally consciously directed to the emotional problems workers were having with the model. At one point, Brahms and the team leaders expressed a concern that the staff was not truly committed. In early 1977, an outside consultant was hired to conduct sessions on the ability to work as a team. A variety of games and exercises, including roleplaying, were used with modest results. Some workers were confronted with their uncooperative behavior and attitudes. In one team, tensions between homemakers and social workers surfaced and were dealt with in a mutually satisfactory fashion.

The problems workers had with convening meetings, monitoring, and contracting were problems not completely soluble through staff training. These problems related to the structure of other agencies, their workers' values, their authority and reward systems, and their relationship to LESFU. Systematic study of these problems was needed before any training was attempted; if this had been done, no doubt it would have been clear that the staff of other agencies required training in the agency's model. Any replication of LESFU will have to concern itself with this issue.

The training curriculum did not develop out of a needs study of the requisites for operationalizing the model; it focused primarily on worker-client interactions. Not enough early emphasis was given to organizational issues that contribute or detract from collaborative efforts. The real value of the training was that it kept morale up and kept people working on the model, at their own pace and style, which was important, given the varied background and limited experience of most of the staff.

Accountability

The accountability system, another facet of agency operation, had an impact like that of training. In the fall of 1976, LESFU began to develop a set of case accountability forms with the help of a consultant. The forms served as a record of the date of the intake interview, when the goal attainment scale was completed, the signing of a contract, and so on.

Brahms devoted a great deal of energy to working with the staff in developing this form (see Table 1) and others. Trial runs were held. Staff members were assured that the purpose of the forms was not to evaluate individual workers but to pick up patterns and problems related to the agency's ability to deliver services. It took well over a year to implement the case-tracking system. Brahms' patient implementation had two effects: It signaled to staff members that, no matter how difficult, the model of service must be followed and it assured them that he was aware of the difficulties in writing contracts and convening meetings and that he appreciated their efforts.

The agency had actually been operating for three years without a regular systematic means of assessing its caseload. Had this system been made operational earlier, there certainly would have been more pressure on an already pressured staff. Without complete and precise data on the results achieved, a more relaxed atmosphere was possible. However, with a tracking system, the agency would have picked up problems with the service model much sooner. Given the nature of the staff's skill and commitment to service rather than to the development of a service model, it is questionable whether problems could have been dealt with more

Table 1. Social Work Associate Case Status Report: High-Risk Cases.

Case Name	Initial Contact Date	Engagement						Service Arrangements							Outcome		
		Client Work Agreement			Goals Set			Convening		Contract			Monitor		Termination Date	Success	Failure
		P	A	O.K.	P	A	O.K.	P	A	P	A	O.K.	P	A			
J.	12/4 /75	1/25	1/25	1/25	2/15	2/15	2/15	2/25	2/25	5/15							
M.	12/25/75	1/25	2/25	2/28	2/15	3/15	3/15	4/15	5/15	6/15	6/30	7/20	8/1	8/1	12/25/76		
W.	2/1 /76	3/1	3/15	3/20	3/30	4/5	4/6	4/20	4/20	5/1	5/10	5/15					
O.	3/1 /76	4/5	4/5	4/20	5/1	5/5	5/15										
K.	4/1 /76	4/30	5/10	5/15	5/5	5/15											

Key: P = Planned date for activity; A = Actual date of activity; O.K. = Team leader approval.

quickly. But without an accountability system, the agency was operating blindly.

Another adaptation that eased the pressure on the workers was a relaxation of the expectations of the results possible with high-risk clients. Workers were to determine high risk by considering a template of the "high-risk family" developed in the training sessions. The template included certain "automatics," such as a family with a child in placement or recently returned from placement, a family with a child involved in the juvenile justice system, and a family suspected of child abuse or maltreatment; there were fewer than ten automatic categories. Families with any one of these characteristics were considered high-risk on the basis of a single category.

Families with none of the automatic indicators were also considered high-risk after an assessment of their problems and strengths. For this assessment, there were a number of high-risk "signals" that workers looked for, including drug or alcohol abuse by a family member, truancy for a school-age child, physical or mental disorder of a family member, overcrowded living conditions, and many other factors that would indicate a highly unstable family situation. Against these signals the worker weighed such strengths as the existence of an extended family to care for the children, a reasonably stable marriage, and the possibility of outlets, such as temporarily sending a child to Puerto Rico. If, despite the strengths encountered, the worker and team leader feel that the family lacks the capacity to care for its children without the support of LESFU, then the family is designated as high-risk and full service to the family is provided by LESFU.

As noted earlier, this designation was not an easy one to make. More importantly, it was very frustrating to work with the high-risk clients because they were at times suspicious and seemingly uncooperative. In 1977, Brahms wrote the following evaluation:

> The Lower East Side Family Union has operated under the assumption that high-risk families can be stabilized and, once themselves stabilized, will become interested in helping their neighbors resolve problems similar to those that they experienced. As their strength and awareness increase, the stabilized families can next be involved in groups working on problems of general com-

munity concern, and finally, in the governance of LESFU itself.

We are concluding that our original assumptions concerning the clients may well have been unrealistic. For one thing, a number of our clients will probably never be stabilized as this word is commonly understood. They are too damaged by the time we reach them and their lives are too crisis-ridden. These crises, which erupt periodically, are extremely disabling. To keep such families together we might have to be prepared to intervene periodically possibly until the youngest child is ready to become independent of his or her parents (by the age of eighteen).

Second, while we may be able to involve some of the families in the steps subsequent to stabilization, most are still struggling to keep their own heads above water. To expect active community participation from these families may not be too realistic. At the LESFU governance level, this holds true as well. Dealing with their own pressures and needs leaves them little time or interest for governing an agency."

This lifted a great deal of pressure from the workers. If clients were not always helped, it was not necessarily the worker's fault.

Perhaps the clearest indication of a relaxation of the original plan, while adhering to its spirit, was the action of the community organizer, Bill Field. After a difficult entry into the agency, he formed a fourth team in an adjacent area; while the team engaged in a variety of self-help programs related to providing tutorial assistance, neighborhood clean-up, job placement, and the like, it also attempted to develop mutual self-help networks among the clients.

The intent was to have a resource file of neighborhood residents with special skills that clients could use. A client with a welfare problem could be put in touch with a neighbor who knew the ins and outs of the welfare system. By early 1978, this file was slowly being developed. Whether or not it leads to a union of families cannot be predicted, but it does indicate the agency's dedication— for which Brahms deserves considerable credit—to the original intent of the project.

This dogged commitment to the service model was also apparent in the work of the more skilled social work associates. There were great variations in quality of work and commitment to the model, but the following family service contract related to alleged child neglect illustrates the potential of the service model.

Family Service Contract

LESFU Social Work Associate: Joy Inteston
Family Name: J.

Family Composition

Mary	Mother	33 years
Anthony	Son	8 years
Harriet	Daughter	7 years
Joseph	Son	6 years
William	Son	4 years
Angelo	Son	2 years
John	Son	2 months

Presenting Problems

Mary J. was referred to the Lower East Side Family Union by Nora Jones of Collegiate House for emergency house-keeping service on December 4, 1975. She was due to give birth and had no one to care for her six children. Mary J. has had difficulty with childrearing tasks. She has had difficulty in getting children off to school on time and keeping medical appointments both for herself and children. Mary J. has serious varicose vein problems in her legs; her condition has worsened with each pregnancy. In November, 1975, Mary J. was reported to Bureau of Child Welfare for alleged neglect. In order to stabilize the family situation, Mary J. will need help in home and time management and childrearing. In addition, she will continue to need the after school program for her three eldest children and a program for the two youngest so that she can devote necessary time to her newborn.

Specific Services to be Provided

1. Sara Ponce on behalf of the visiting nurse service, has agreed to continue to provide the J. family with a visiting nurse, Johnson, about once every three weeks for the next three

months. She will specifically see that Mary J. follows the doctor's advice for taking care of her varicose veins and the children's ailments.

2/28/76   *Sara Ponce*
Date   Visiting Nurse Service

2. Jenny Pirate, Social Worker, Pediatrics, on behalf of Bellevue Hospital has agreed to secure a part time housekeeper for the J. Family (to have begun on February 16, 1976), and will follow-up to insure that this service is rendered. Pirate will coordinate the medical appointments for the family and in advance will notify Isabel Nunez, Family Worker, Headstart Program of Collegiate Settlement House. Pirate will coordinate the transfer of Mary J.'s medical records after Mary J. has her postpartum examination at St. Vincent's Hospital.

2/8/76   *Jenny Pirate*
Date   Social Worker

3. Isabel Nunez, Family Worker, Headstart Program, on behalf of Collegiate House, has agreed to provide counseling around concrete needs, excluding mental health counseling for Mary J. since Joseph and Anthony have been accepted into this program effective March 17, 1976. Nunez will work with Mary J. to see that she meets all the medical appointments of which Mrs. Pirate will inform them. Nunez will call Mary J. each time the youngsters miss two consecutive days in the Headstart Program.

3/26/76   *Isabel Nunez*
Date   Family Worker, Headstart

4. Carole Johny, Director, Headstart Program on behalf of Collegiate House, has agreed to let Ronnie Fish, Educational Director for the program, meet with Joy Inteston of the Lower East Side Family Union and Holmes, Director of Step One Day Care of Bellevue to determine where Anthony's educational needs can best be met, keeping in mind that Mary J. prefers that Anthony attend Collegiate's Headstart.

4/22/76   *Carole Johny*
Date   Director, Headstart Program

5. Collegiate Settlement's League for Child Care will provide after school daycare to William, Harriet, and John J.

We will inform Joy Inteston of the status and progress of the
children and of our contacts with Mary J. regarding these three
of her children.

4/27/76   *Paul Green*
Date   Director, League for Child Care

6. Joy Inteston, Social Work Associate on behalf of the
Lower East Side Family Union will be responsible for coordinating and convening another meeting of the client and service
providers in two-and-one-half to three months. Inteston will
monitor the contract to insure that all commitments are kept
and that all services in the plan are provided.

2/25/76   *Joy Inteston*
Date   Social Work Associate

7. Mary J. has agreed to make an immediate appoint-
ment at St. Vincent's Hospital for a postpartum examination.
She has agreed to send Anthony and Joseph to University Settlement House's Headstart Program, and to call Nunez whenever
these children cannot attend. Also, if one child is sick, she has
agreed to send the other one.

3/16/76   *Mary J.*
Date   Client

Judith Ash once quipped that she knew that a demonstration
project had to proceed slowly, but did it have to be slowed down?
Given the problems with the complexity of the model and the staff's
lack of sophistication, the answer at LESFU is yes, it had to be
slowed down. She also questioned the board's function. At LESFU,
the board knew very little about what was happening at the agency.
Without adequate information, they could not account for the
agency's activities. They did hire Brahms, whose patient devotion to
the project kept it moving in its demonstration direction.

If the board had known what was happening, could the work
of the project been speeded up or carried out more efficiently? This
question, still open to debate, relates to a general question of
whether boards can effectively account for agencies. Brown (1975,
pp. 277–278) comments on this issue:

The technical content of administration is increasing, as is the complexity of the language used in

analytic policy making. The layman . . . needs to know
enough about the subject to be able to ask the right questions. If he intervenes too often, he will paralyze and
frustrate the work of specialist officers; if he does not
intervene enough he might as well not be there. It is not
absurd to have training programs for laymembers of au-
thorities and boards. But the informed tend to become
the committed. We may need informed laymen to keep
an eye on the specialists, and uninformed laymen to keep
an eye on the informed. . . . We need a series of inter-
mediaries and interpreters, and this is at least part of the
role of laymembers of [boards] . . .

    None of the devices we have been exploring works
terribly well. The representative system is unimpressive
except when it is prodded into action by a group of
activists. Cause groups are ineffective unless they can
attract the attention of public representatives. But they
add up to a complex system which may work better than
any of its parts. The operationally important form of
accountability is the mixture of formal devices and con-
ventions, rooted in our political culture, for publicizing
the workings of a system, so that those who are interested
can spot errors and imbalances and appeal to constitu-
tional rules and cultural norms to have them put right.
The touchstone is perhaps neither formal accountability
nor participation, but openness.

Besides inadequate consideration of the form and procedures
of board functioning, too little attention in program design has been
given to reducing tension. Most designs seem to operate on the assumption that if the design is sound there will be little tension
among the staff, department, and the agency's goals. It is more
likely that considerable tension is inevitable in complex organizations and programs; their design should include mechanisms for
handling this tension. At LESFU, tension-reducing mechanisms
emerged gradually in response to board versus staff conflicts and
difficulties in operationalizing the model. Whether or not these
were the most efficient or effective mechanisms possible under the
circumstances remains a moot question.

    Similarly, LESFU was fortunate in not creating tensions
where there was no inherent cause for them. Had Brahms imposed

the case-tracking system without sensitivity to the staff's concern
about evaluation, he probably would have created a ritual of the
staff following the service model without concern for actual results.
Progress in the records is not always progress in reality.

The crucial factor for an agency administrator is not to
attempt to reduce tension per se but to use tension to promote organizational ends. The key to making this possible is keeping communication lines open between those involved in setting and implementing policy so that tensions are actually shared—the various
parties involved understand the pressures each operates under. Tensions are merely recognized when each party knows that something
is wrong.

Shared tensions or mutual understanding will not single-
handedly lead to actions that will satisfy everyone or even to good
problem solutions; knowledge and skill are also needed. What it will
do is alert an organization to all the ramifications of various problems and solutions. At LESFU, as Table 2 illustrates, a number of
unshared tensions piled up over the years.

Although there are different tensions, as the table shows, two
types are crucial for administrators and policy makers to share: 1)
tension generated in clients deriving from discrepancies between
what clients expect and what they receive, and 2) tension generated
by the staff resulting from differences between what they are asked
to do and what they think they should do.

Brahms was able to promote more mutual understanding at
LESFU by formalizing the authority system so that all staff knew
specifically what was expected of them, acknowledging that the
SWA job was very difficult, allowing criticism and negative feelings
to be expressed at training sessions, and keeping everyone aware of
the pressures on the agency while making consistent and fair decisions that were responsive to pressures other than his own.

In organizational life, it is difficult to have all parties understand the pressures each one operates under. Some pressures—such
as desires for status, personal rivalries, and job insecurities—are
hidden for fear of what might happen if they were known. Other
pressures—desires to expand departmental budgets, interests in
more autonomy, and desires to reduce the power of others—are
purposefully hidden in order to achieve certain ends. Such pressures

Table 2. Unshared Tensions

Source of Pressure	Date	Operational Pressure	Lack of Understanding Between Groups	Consequence
Sunnie Gold	1972–1974	desire that board be comprised mainly of local residents	clients-board	opportunities unexplored for citizen participation beyond decision making; union of families does not develop
Staff	1974	desire to serve all in need	staff-board	conflicts over research versus service exacerbated
Social work associates	1974	desire to do their job with the techniques they are most comfortable with	LESFU-other agencies	a confused image of LESFU is projected to other agencies
Team leaders	1975	wish to avoid community organizing	staff-staff	new community worker flounders; family union never develops
Staff	1975	desire to not participate in social history process	staff-board	feedback system never develops
State researcher	1975	desire to restrict service to conform to research design	staff-board	staff afraid those in need will not get service; research felt to be a burden
Social historian	1975	desire to observe worker-client interactions	staff-social historian	staff passively resists participation in social history
Staff of contract agencies	1976	desire to not attend convenings or write contracts	LESFU-other agencies	resist cooperation with LESFU
Team leaders	1976	desire board members to make their settlements cooperate with LESFU	staff-board	team leaders question legitimacy of board

and conflicts highlight the importance of organizational leadership
in expanding the degree to which tensions are shared.

Although the formal communication system among the
board, administrators, and staff was flawed, LESFU evolved a back-
up system. Brahms felt free to call on Rue when he had questions
and problems. The team leaders showed silent support for Brahms
at board meetings but knew they could speak freely in their weekly
meetings with him. Gold allowed negative feelings to surface from
workers and team leaders at training sessions; at the same time she
insisted on a high caliber of work.

There were breakdowns, over an extended period with some
issues, such as those related to client perception of service, but the
communication system at LESFU was fairly open. This adds credence to Brown's comment about "openness" being the touchstone of
an accountability system. It is also likely that the key to effective management is an open approach, rather than authoritarian or democratic
styles, which can both be closed; decisions can be made by voting
or by fiat without any real understanding of the pressures under
which various organizational participants operate.

Open management is not simply concerned with revealing
and resolving organizational tensions. It may even impose certain
tensions. LESFU's accountability system (Chapter Eight describes
it in detail) created a great deal of tension. Goals and results were
clearly visible; they no longer could be avoided. To use this tension
to promote organizational ends, a communication system is needed
that allows discussion of questions and disagreements as well as of
facts and figures.

By giving a picture of results and accomplishments, the accountability system puts a parameter on disagreements that otherwise might escalate into organizational disruptions or antagonisms
of a personal, ideological, or professional nature. The communication system makes the accountability system real by providing an
outlet for frustrations and ideas. Without such an outlet, it is unlikely that solutions to organizational problems can be found. By late
1977, LESFU's accountability and communication systems were well
on the way toward working together.

7

Successes and Failures
in Integrating Services
and Helping Families

The processes by which LESFU was developed—the behaviors, motivations, and goals of various actors—have been analyzed in previous chapters. Similarly, products of its planning process, values, theories, and assumptions underlying the choice of clients, funding mechanisms, and the service model have been scrutinized. This chapter focuses on the agency's performance—to what extent it carried out its plans, what was its impact, and what was learned about the service model.

As of January 1978, the agency's current high-risk caseload was reported as shown in Table 3. It is not possible to prove how many of the families would have placed their children or been forced to place them without the service of LESFU. The agency also served numerous cases that did not qualify as high-risk.

According to Rue, placing a child in foster care can cost from

This chapter was written in collaboration with Marie Weil.

Table 3. Sources of the LESFU High-Risk Cases

Source	Number of cases referred
Contract Agencies with Board Representation	
Special Services for Children	14
Gouverneur Hospital	10
Collegiate Settlement	5
Monroe	2
Glory Street Settlement	2
Harold Street Settlement	1
Total	34
Other Agencies	
Board of Education	12
Department of Social Services	4
MFY-Legal Services	3
Police	3
New York Infirmary	2
Bellevue Hospital	2
Manhattan Development Center	2
12 agencies provided us with one case each	12
Total	40
Nonagency Sources	
Outreach and walk-in	29
Client referral	5
Total	34
Grand Total	108

$5 thousand to $40 thousand a year, depending on the quality of care. The Family Union preventive work costs from $12 hundred to $15 hundred per family per year; although this figure does not include the cost of services provided by other agencies or the cost of their workers' time spent at contracting and monitoring meetings, LESFU is still probably cheaper, even if the emotional and social costs of breaking up a family are not considered.

Implementing the Model

The agency had not fully developed its capacity to utilize the service model by early 1978, but a great deal had been learned about its implementation, enabling the agency to further the model's development. Other agencies wishing to experiment with it should be able to start with a solid base of knowledge.

The LESFU model, in contrast to traditional casework models, "starts with a conception of child welfare casework as a managerial function, gathering information and setting a process for decision making, planning toward definite goals, analysis and establishment of specific tasks (related) to goal achievement, coordination of people and services, and developing fundamental agreements and contracts with parents (by providing) a major role for parents in task definition and accomplishment" ("A Managerial Model . . . ," 1976, p. 21). As such, LESFU was concerned with changing client and worker relationships as well as the relationships of agencies providing services to clients.

The managerial function developed out of disenchantment with the clinical casework model, where administrative roles are acknowledged but emphasis is given to the treatment aspects of the child welfare worker. The disenchantment was related to "a high percent of children spending many years drifting in foster care, low levels of parent involvement, absence of planning, inability to set and communicate goals, inappropriate placement, and violation of civil rights" (1976, p. 21). LESFU clearly addressed these problems in its service model.

Outreach. The original intent of the agency was to recruit high-risk clients—those who had severe problems and were not currently receiving services from any existing agencies. However, high-risk clients were the most difficult to work with, as their name implies. As one worker observed, a person who has all of the problems that we are concerned about is not about to step forward on the basis of a flyer or a knock on the door. Team leader Sue Taste noted that "You go out and get some more people who are resistant to your work." This recruitment inevitably resulted in frustration.

In any system, ways of accomplishing a task without complying with procedures generally emerge if the procedures are considered onerous. For example, it was possible for homemakers to bring in clients, but, as William Penn, one of the social workers, noted, "this often sets up a situation where service is given before there is real clarity about just what the problems are."

Penn felt that, at one time or another, all families with

children touch base with an agency and certainly with the schools. Thus LESFU's outreach efforts might have been better concentrated on working with the staffs of these agencies on different ways of referring clients to LESFU and on different ways of working with clients who tend to disappear after an initial contact with an agency. Such clients often make the headlines about child abuse and neglect. However, having workers who resided in the community, speaking at community meetings, sending newsletters, and putting posters in grocery stores played an important part in the agency's outreach efforts. A balance between direct and indirect efforts to reach clients is required.

Engagement. In this precontract phase of the model, the worker and client agree on what problems are to be worked on and the mutual responsibilities of each. This is a crucial step, for if clients are not committed to problem definition and resolution, it is unlikely that any lasting gain will derive from the services offered. The fact that LESFU workers had to develop a work agreement assisted the engagement. A worker from another agency stated that the LESFU workers were extremely good at isolating specific problems without forgetting the scope of the clients' problems. No doubt the structure helped both clients and workers avoid being overwhelmed by the enormity of their tasks. The agency's easy access to clients and the workers who spoke languages other than English aided engagement. In addition, the social work associates could negotiate complex agency systems for clients. Crisis intervention was the way of life for the agency; most clients quickly got some assistance.

Perhaps the major new development in the engagement process that differentiated the LESFU approach from that of other agencies was the homemaker and social work associate pair. Two workers acting in unison reinforced each other. They also provided the client with two role models needed frequently in crisis-ridden families. The homemaker acts as a model for care of children and home by making the home a habitable and more comfortable place and by handling such daily life chores as shopping. The SWA provides a problem-solving model, which the client can emulate. Additionally, having the HMK in the home during the day and working with the parents and children was a valuable addition to assessment of client concerns, commitment, and change. An article written by Carlina Wills, a city homemaker assigned to Team Three, illustrates why this was possible at LESFU; it also reveals problems with the way homemakers were used in the city services.

There is an enormous difference in the home-maker's task at LESFU and at the Department of Social Services (DSS). I have been working as a homemaker at the Family Union almost two years now, and before that, as a homemaker at DSS. Several factors account for the difference.

Homemakers at LESFU work directly with a team leader who oversees an entire team. At DSS, a director supervises a field worker, who in turn supervises the homemakers. I have found that direct supervision of homemakers by a team leader . . . eliminates the "little bosses" and creates a better relationship among members of the entire team.

Another factor is that LESFU's homemakers receive more training. . . . At DSS, training focuses on duties in the home of the client, where the worker is to perform tasks until the family can take them over. At the Family Union, the focus is different. It is to learn to build a strong relationship with the family to motivate them to change. [We] train clients in child care and home management so that eventually they will be able and will desire to do these things for themselves.

A LESFU homemaker gets involved in all aspects of delivering services to a family, [such as] helping the family assess their needs in homemaking. At DSS, this important decision is made by a supervisor. The home-makers have little if any input in deciding what services are appropriate for a family—and, of course, they are in an excellent position to know. In an average week, as well as caring for our clients, we . . . pull case records to get a better picture of the family's situation. (City homemakers never see a case record.) In addition, we will talk over cases at meetings, attend training sessions, and discuss cases with members of other LESFU teams. Through the log we keep, the supervisors will know what went on that week . . . It answers the questions "Did your plans work out?" and "Was there cooperation on the client's part?"

Another important difference is that the Family Union's homemakers work with a contract. . . . It eliminates misunderstandings of the homemaker's role in the home. At DSS, there is an oral agreement for the work assignment. It is seldom carried out and easily misinterpreted.

I hope DSS will take a good look at the LESFU model because it has a lot to offer in motivating clients, and it gives a homemaker incentive to do a better job.

Engagement of clients is the most subtle part and in many ways the linchpin of the LESFU process. Besides the HMK and SWA pairing, crisis intervention, and immediate concrete assistance, many clients responded to the feasibility of LESFU's work. The agency did not vaguely promise it would do everything; it promised to develop a work agreement quickly, stating specifically what it and the client would do. Starting when feasible with the problems the clients were most concerned about—tailoring the agency to client concerns rather than vice versa—helped immeasurably in engaging the clients.

Work Agreement. The worker and client's agreement on the goals of the immediate services to be rendered, the tasks that each must accomplish, and their priorities is formalized in a goal attainment scale, which establishes success indicators for various tasks.

Following the agreement that sets out what services will be sought, the social work associate is responsible for connecting the client to needed services. Because of the nature of many clients' problems, the provision of some services often preceded the development of a work agreement. This process, although logically following the intake interview, was in practice quite problematic. The frequent crises in clients' lives sometimes made work agreements and the goal attainment scales obsolete, almost before they were written. The ritual of filling out the agreement and scale after the fact in some situations confused clients. Also, it was difficult to set realistic short-term goals since much of the service would be given by other agencies to which the client often had not yet been referred.

Most social work associates felt that clients in a state of crisis were willing to sign the work agreement and the goal attainment scale but did not see the purpose of it even though the clients said they did. This lack of understanding indicated real problems in the engagement of clients. Some workers noted that goal attainment scaling focused their work and made them aware of whether they were on the same wavelength as the client. It also gave them a tool for evaluating their progress with particular clients. The degree to which clients should be involved in goal and task specification should be determined by the nature of the client and the presenting problems. The actual written goal attainment scale, with specification of good, fair, and poor results, was too cumbersome in many cases given the nature of the client's problems. Flexibility in utilizing the scale and developing the work agreements is crucial for maintaining their value.

Family Service Contract. Following the work agreement, which specified problems and duties, the worker prepared the client for the family service contract meeting, so that the client was aware of each agency's services. In developing an effective family service contract, careful preparation of the client and agency representatives for the contract meeting is critical. The formal steps at LESFU were as follows: "The preparation of the agencies should include discussion of family needs and priorities, outline of total service plan, specific statement of needs from each particular agency with prior negotiation if necessary regarding what services can be offered, their frequency, initiation, timing, duration, and depth. The names of workers to be involved in contract performance should be secured along with specification of responsibilities. Prior agreement should also be secured with each agency regarding the form of feedback from worker to worker and client to worker and the form and frequency of contract monitoring."

The LESFU worker's preparation for the contract conference should have been so thorough that there are no surprises for any party at the conference. Any new circumstances may be discussed at the conference and, if a mutual decision is possible, be included in the initial contract. If a decision cannot be reached, the difficulty and steps to remedy it should be noted in writing. The worker should send a draft of the contract to the agencies in question prior to the contract meeting. This will provide a chance for any needed changes and will allow the LESFU worker to read the completed contract and obtain signatures at the contract meeting.

Brahms pointed out that this formal, slow, and meticulous process was initially necessary to educate agency staffs about a family service contract; they needed time to get attuned to it—to read, discuss, and ask questions about it. The key process is developing trust. After several successful contracts, the procedures could be altered and adjusted as called for by particular situations.

William Penn, one of the most effective SWAs, describes adaptations he introduced as well as his view of the contracts:

> The contract is a burden to me but is also a lifesaver. Clients often complain that I didn't follow through on my commitments. When this occurs, I can always point to the contract. Social workers have a bad habit of moving ahead of the client. The client never agrees or fully understands the social worker's point of view and concern for him, and vice versa. The contract keeps everyone honest.
>
> It is not that social workers don't do anything, it is that they try to do everything. In that sense, the contract is very helpful, as it forces me to think about what I can really do and what can really be done in a realistic time period. It took me a long time to develop the "tricks" to writing contracts.
>
> There's always the issue in the minds of the representatives of the other agencies, "Who are you to be asking me to sign this?" One has to be very careful about the words that are used. It is dangerous to say in the contract that you are going to monitor the doctors and the lawyers as well as other social workers. I don't type up a contract before the meeting. I fill it in right after the meeting. The idea that you can go there with a written contract and have professionals review it is absolutely in error, at least from the point of view of a nonprofessional convening the meeting. I have found that professionals are willing to sign what they have said, so I merely fill in what they have said.

Penn's success stemmed in part from his understanding of the subtle dynamics of contract meetings. For example, bringing the client to the point where a problem or series of problems is recognized is quite a job, but at a contract meeting it appears that this procedure did not require much work at all. Thus, at his contract meetings, Penn had the client say what the social worker did—how long it took and what the process was. He felt that this legitimized his role as a convener of the contract meeting. Penn also was attuned to clients' feelings about meetings:

> Some agencies' representatives talk about clients as if they weren't at the meeting. In these situations I always turn back to the client. Does she understand? Does she agree? . . . This [must] be done because after the meeting you get, "How come you let those people say all those things about me?" You're going to have trouble helping such a client if this is how she feels after a contract meeting.
>
> If I know some person at the contract meeting will frighten the client, I try to get the client to meet this professional, a doctor, a lawyer, before the meeting. Unfortunately, some clients get overwhelmed by the enormity of their problems, when it is clearly spelled out at a contract meeting. This really has to be gauged before the meeting. It is absolutely essential to talk to the client immediately after the meeting. I generally go home with the client.

Penn's comments clearly illustrate the complexity of contracting. No formula or sequential set of procedures completely covers all contingencies. What did emerge at LESFU was a contracting process closely related to the ideas of structural service delivery developed by Middleman and Goldberg (1974).

Aside from diagnosis and basic treatment skills necessary to develop rapport with the client and engagement for needed change, SWAs assume a set of escalating roles to secure cooperation and service commitment from other agencies. Middleman and Goldberg classify the activities necessary to assure agency cooperation by the following role behaviors: conferee, broker, mediator, and advocate.

These roles are related to the degree and type of influence needed to secure service for clients—rationality, rewards, and punishment. Since continued relationships with agencies are important, a

worker must judge how best to gain and maintain agency cooperation. If agencies and clients are in general agreement about what
must be done, the social work associate can play the role of conferee,
focusing the discussion and clarifying the decisions. If clients are
not able to clearly articulate their needs, the worker may have to
act as a broker, stating precisely what is needed. When there are
conflicts between agencies or between clients and agencies, workers
may have to play a mediating role, suggesting how each might
mutually benefit from some action. And, at other times, they may
have to advocate forcefully and enter an antagonistic relationship
with agencies.

Middleman and Goldberg suggest that workers should
proceed on the assumption of least contest, assuming the role of
conferee before broker, broker before mediator, and mediator before
advocate. If agencies can be rationally persuaded, why threaten a
public dispute?

With some agencies, more was required to gain their cooperation than clarification of the social work associate role. Brahms
felt that it was necessary for LESFU to develop different approaches
and perhaps different contracts with certain legal and mental health
organizations.

Working with Legal and Mental Health Services. Generally,
lawyers working in legal aid organizations state that their responsibility is to represent the interests of the natural parents in retaining
a child in the home or securing return of the child from placement.
They said that they would never divulge damaging information—
for example, evidence of abuse or neglect—about a client to a social
agency or to the court.

However, LESFU is bound, as are all social agencies, to
report instances of suspected neglect or abuse to Special Services for
Children, but it can continue work to preserve the family unit and
prevent foster placement. Only when other resources are exhausted
or seem ineffective in exerting positive change would LESFU urge
removing the child from the home by the public agency. (This has
occurred in only twelve cases during 1976 and eleven during 1977.)

Practical problems result from different professional stances
towards confidentiality. A primary disagreement is the question of
who is the client. Legal aid associations were often anxious to refer

their clients—parents—to LESFU for service but were unwilling to acknowledge fully why the service was required if the problem involved abuse or neglect. LESFU was concerned about what might happen to a child after taking on a case before developing enough rapport and trust to find out all the relevant details. The issues were responsibility and accountability. Some LESFU staff members felt that the offer of such a referral was not collaborative and that it caused real problems for the agency.

A different issue involves cooperation or the lack of it between legal agencies and public social agencies, such as Legal Aid versus Special Services for Children (SSC), which view themselves and often are in adversarial relationships. SSC has a primary obligation to protect the safety and health of children who are allegedly abused or neglected, and the Legal Aid lawyer is obligated to advocate for his client. LESFU had several contract meetings where both agencies were present; the adversarial stance of their representatives made collaboration difficult. Brahms concluded that in such situations LESFU may have to mediate the positions of other agencies while trying to provide the best possible and most constructive service for their defined client, the family, accepting the fact that other agencies may not take that total view. LESFU would have to hold separate meetings to mediate between conflicting organizations before the client and other service agencies could be brought in or at least forewarn everyone as to the expected problems.

Other problems developed in working with agencies that offered mental health services. First, the whole area of gaining clients' acceptance of this service was charged. Some SWAs were reluctant to refer clients and some were not equipped to judge whether or not clients needed the service.

The mental health agencies that worked best with LESFU shared its view of focusing on clients' strengths, emphasizing mutuality, and utilizing a task orientation. "We are going to work on how you discipline your child rather than work on your aggressive feelings" expresses this approach. Nevertheless, some workers had difficulty telling clients that they needed therapy. For example, a SWA sent one mother to Harold Street, a settlement with a mental health clinic, noting that she and her child needed therapy; the mother showed up, saying to the receptionist, "Somebody here is supposed to play with my child." Although intentional or unintentional resistance on the client's part may have been in operation, it is likely that the Family Union worker did not do a thorough job of client preparation.

The problems with many mental health agencies revolved primarily around disagreements over function and priorities. The difficulties with the clinic at Monroe House were more acute, although symptomatic. The clinic director saw therapy as the central service that all clients needed. She felt that the centrality of the "therapeutic relationship" required her workers to be case managers, while the LESFU would provide homemaker and other concrete services.

This difference over what was most important for the client reflected a deep difference over the nature of therapy. Are the therapeutic and diagnostic techniques of the workers pivotal? Or is the emphasis on maximum client participation the crucial dimension of service? In addition to this disagreement, or perhaps as part of it, were complaints from mental health workers that it was demeaning to a client to sit in on contract meetings; not everything should be shared with the client. They also thought that SWAs could not adequately deal with family needs or future plans because they could not diagnose the psychosocial problems of the family.

Besides professional conflicts, there were many problems of a more practical nature. Attending meetings was very time consuming. The top priority is to provide services, and in many situations the services had actually been offered for some time, so it seemed meaningless to have a contract. The social work associates were often confronted with the demand to "just bring the clients over and we'll give them service, but we're not going to come to a meeting." Not surprisingly, some of the greatest problems came up in dealing with paraprofessionals in other agencies. They viewed the LESFU workers as "taking over their cases." In some ways they often viewed their worth in terms of providing many services for their clients. The contracting model tended to take them away from center stage and to make them accountable to a vague and potentially threatening source.

Role Strains. Another difficulty emerged from some of the

early contract meetings, where two departments of a settlement—
for example, the counseling and the remedial education department—were both called on to provide services. It turned out that
these departments had trouble coordinating services between
themselves. The assumption that the problems of cooperation are
exclusively related to interorganizational dilemmas, that is, status
and control, is not altogether true. In fact, the *intra*organizational
difficulties may be as potent. Who can ensure that two or three
departments of one organization cooperate internally?

As Sue Taste said, "You have to change the client and
change the agency at the same time and that is difficult." An example of a complicated agency for the workers was Special Services
for Children (SSC). LESFU referred neglect cases to SSC, the
public agency for protecting the rights of abused children. An
arrangement was worked out with a special unit in SSC to accept
LESFU's referrals and to coordinate their efforts with LESFU's
efforts. Unfortunately, the arrangements with SSC were worked out
with the higher levels of the organization. Some workers in the
special unit were not willing to cooperate or to accept LESFU's
judgment about neglect. This conflict occurred because the top
leaders of SSC did not understand the pressures and constraints
under which workers in the special unit operated.

First, these workers were overworked. Second, this was an
extremely stressful job—taking children away from their parents. To
handle their overwork and frustration, special unit workers followed
the policy that if the family court was involved with some other
member of the family, then SSC did not have to be involved in any
other case of neglect in that family; they merely referred it to the
court. Since this was the situation with many neglect cases, cooperation between LESFU and SSC depended on the interest and concern of SSC workers.

Similar situations occurred with other cooperating agencies.
LESFU agreed to have contracts with the executives of these
agencies, but the staff was not involved in discussing this arrangement. The executives had limited knowledge of the inner-workings
of their various departments; they did not see that they had to
exercise leadership in analyzing the internal effects of a contract
with another agency or series of agencies. Their workers tended to

resist the contracting idea, primarily because it put severe constraints and pressures on them. It changed their reward system, their ability to control their work, and their sense of purpose and professional competence. If LESFU is replicated, more effort must be put into understanding the internal ramifications of interagency cooperation.

Sex and Ethnicity. At different points, each of the primary groups served—Hispanics, Blacks, and Chinese—was reported as not wanting to sign their names to anything. For Spanish-speaking and Chinese clients, the reason reported was that in these cultures one's word is one's bond and to ask for a signature was an indication of lack of faith. For Blacks, the reason reported was negative experience with signing anything.

It may be that the ethnic preferences were related more to class income and, in some instances, peasant orientation than to clearly discrete cultural factors, but these differences were perceived as ethnic by workers. There was general agreement among staff members that Chinese clients were the most loath to accept welfare and would be reduced to extreme states of deprivation before seeking help. This was attributed to fear of "losing face," although it may also have been related to lack of knowledge of available services, since most Chinese clients were recent immigrants from Hong Kong. Spanish-speaking clients were often described as more dependent on workers and wanting to have someone to help them deal with other agencies. In both these instances, real or individually exaggerated problems of language barriers account for some of the behavior noted.

Blacks have a long history of social agency relationships. By and large, they were reported to be extremely suspicious and think that all agencies are in collusion. Signing a contract without working this feeling out can be a great mistake. From past experience, they have learned how to deal with agencies that they feel are in collusion, by manipulating and pitting one agency against another and one worker against another worker; this has been their means of survival. These generalizations were stated in various forms by workers of various ethnic backgrounds. However, a reading of cases uncovered quite a number of Black clients unaware of services and unskilled at manipulating the system to secure services. Nevertheless, longevity of residence and language factors may grant some credence to the generalizations made by the workers regarding the Black clients.

Similarly, most workers felt that special care had to be given to commitments made by females. Their husbands, if present, tended to resent the power given to women to determine things.

Clients and Contracts. The clients' views of contracting provide different perspectives to consider. Most clients were frightened by the prospect of a formal meeting with representatives from a variety of agencies. Preparation, as noted earlier, was important. Some clients objected to "all those people knowing my business," while others responded favorably to meetings of service providers called by the social work associates. A meeting of four or five workers was tangible evidence to the client that in fact people were concerned. This added inducement was helpful in promoting client self-help. As one client said, "If these people are willing to do so much for me then I should be willing to do something for myself." Clients also felt safe with the contracts; they knew who was going to do what.

One of the main reasons for developing contracts was the desire to help clients learn what agencies are able to and willing to do for and with them. The model of convening and contracting provided an opportunity for clients to see processes of discussion, with disagreement and resolution, and gave them an opportunity to observe how they could hold agencies accountable. For clients in troubled families, this was probably their first experience with a model of problem solving that was open and susceptible to some control.

The whole LESFU approach is one that the client can observe and participate in to experience the activities of the LESFU workers as a style and strategy that they can emulate. This type of role modeling is probably strengthened by the frequent ethnic similarities among workers and clients; LESFU workers were considered part of the community.

There is no systematic evidence on the model's effects on clients. Workers were generally convinced that, with adequate preparation, most clients benefited from the sense of security that the contract conveyed. They felt the model worked best for clients able to see help as more than a one-time affair. The LESFU approach does not ensure growth, but it provides an opportunity for it to occur. This is achieved by keeping the reality perceived by the client at the forefront, providing for crisis intervention and help, limiting client hustling and manipulation of one agency against another, supplying an arena for mutual dialogue and questioning of the agency, client, and worker, offering clients role models to emulate, and clarifying the dimensions of problems and solutions for clients.

Client independence—teaching clients to take care of themselves and their families—was LESFU's desired outcome. It was difficult to develop a systematic policy on how to handle clients who did not fulfill their commitments. Workers had varying opinions on the subject. Penn said, "The rules and policies should not be so steadfast that you actually deny service." He felt clients go through a testing period. Persistence in pointing out the consequences of the client's part of the contract fulfillment was necessary. He was reluctant to deny services. Another social work associate said, "There should be only so much you should do; it's demeaning to the family if you try to do too much," suggesting that at some point service should be denied if clients did not fulfill their commitments. Some SWAs were ambivalent about whether to deny service or not. One said, "I feel guilty that I'm not engaging a person, but then I know that there are others who need my help."

Approximately 12 percent of the caseload was actually closed out, a result of clients who did not respond to repeated calls or who simply drifted away or moved out of the neighborhood. A larger percentage did not fulfill all or part of their contract commitments, but no consistent policy was developed at LESFU to deal with this issue.

In a rigorous study of contracting in another agency, Rhodes (1977) suggests certain solutions to the problems LESFU encountered. She notes that the workers dominated the contracting process and developed contracts too quickly, thus limiting the possibility of mutual client involvement. She suggests that mutual interaction and feedback should be emphasized by elaborating the contracting process as a sequence of steps involving negotiation between a worker and a client over time.

The LESFU experience also indicates that there are times when contracts should not be attempted, especially in the following situations: a crisis is so overwhelming that the client cannot participate at a convening, there is no long-term need for service, an agency is overcommitted, ongoing conflicts between provider agencies limit their ability to formally work together, and the agencies, perspectives, and concerns involved are so numerous that agreements must be worked out in private.

Terry Windward of Team Three concluded that flexibility tempered by reason was important in fitting the model to the clients. "With some things you have to say O.K., we are not going to use this even though it is part of the model, but there should be justification for this decision. If you're not going to have a contract, or if you're not going to do a goal attainment, or you're not going to reconvene, . . . the worker has to justify why not."

Monitoring. At LESFU, overseeing and renegotiating contracts was called *monitoring.* The procedure for and frequency of contract monitoring was discussed at the convening meeting and was part of the signed agreement. Aside from formal monitoring, feedback mechanisms were used to develop a failsafe provision of services. For example, if children are enrolled in a daycare program, it should be specified that, if they miss a certain number of consecutive days or days out of any one week, the LESFU worker will be informed; additionally, it will be understood which agency has the responsibility to check with the client for possible problems.

At the contract conference, the SWA ensures that the clients, as well as agency personnel, understand mutual obligations and reporting procedures. Periodic assessment should be made of family progress (at a minimum of sixty to ninety days) to determine the status of contract implementation. At these intervals, it may be necessary to reframe some objectives and goals to fit changed circumstances. This check every two months with the family and agencies should provide the necessary corrective and feedback mechanism for contract operation.

A number of issues were at play in monitoring contracts. Staff members were often involved in coordinating representatives from as many as eight or nine agencies, representing a wide variety of services—housing, daycare, medical, psychiatric, and mental health services. This variety meant that staff had to cope with assorted perspectives of the client and the nature of service and quite different approaches to work and status. Developing agreements might not be particularly difficult in terms of available services, but developing a consensus regarding the client's needs and a treatment plan was often more complicated; it had to grow out of the monitoring process.

Monitoring seemed to depend more often on the personality of the workers than on the model of work. The main dilemma for workers was maintaining cooperation while ensuring that services promised were in fact delivered. At one point, the word *monitoring* was actually dropped in favor of *follow-up,* on the assumption that monitoring was too threatening to other agencies, as it was. Workers from other agencies reportedly said, "You mean you are going to determine whether therapy is helping the client?" when LESFU workers only asked if the client was coming to the therapy sessions. Other agencies' workers sometimes asked, "Who are you to see if I am delivering my agency's service?" and implied or stated that their professional and academic training made them superior. Sometimes they implied that LESFU's monitoring duplicated their own effort and was a waste of time; sometimes there was outright hostility at infringement on their turf, and at other times a passive acceptance of another "intrusion" on the case.

However, some LESFU workers found positive reactions to the monitoring situation. Staff members from other agencies were often pleased and relieved that the contract specified that the LESFU worker was to be contacted to meet with the client and agency and to redefine situations and solve problems at particular points or breakdowns.

Working out difficulties between other agencies and clients often fell to the Family Union worker, who had to explain, for example, why particular medical tests were important to a child's health or why visits to a therapist were valuable. The increasing complexity of a service—from daycare to mental health on an ascending scale of complexity—made for increased difficulty in monitoring.

Family Union workers found it difficult to monitor mental health or psychiatric services offered to clients. How does one monitor the effectiveness or effect of psychological or psychiatric counseling? Here, in a profound way, the issues of credentials and status appeared. Workers often found that psychiatrists who were willing to meet with clients, workers, and other agencies would do so only in their own offices. Some clients were genuinely fearful and unwilling to let other agencies know that they or their children were receiving mental health services. Some enterprising workers worked out contracts separately with other agencies and with mental health services. As Penn stated, "Why should all those other agencies have to know her business if she doesn't want them to?" This situation raises the tricky issue of confidentiality for clients versus collaboration in the client's interest. Must *everyone* know *everything?* If so, how is confidentiality maintained? If not, on what basis are exclusionary decisions made?

There were other problems in monitoring mental health services. Unless marked change appears in a client's outward behavior, it is difficult to determine what is happening with the therapy. The client may be benefiting from it but may not feel helped. Access to records was not granted to Family Union workers, so estimations of a client's progress were based on observations of overt client behavior or reports from the therapist. The subjectivity of mental health services posed a difficult task for Family Union workers when they were asked to monitor them.

Different styles of monitoring, along with different styles of work, developed. In the predominantly Chinese team, relations with other agencies and monitoring often depended on the skills and good graces of the worker. Within this team, family and community relations were extremely important. This did not affect who was given service but did affect how it was given and secured. A cousin could be relied on to ensure that a client was taken care of properly, but this personal use of relationships hardly fits into a contract model of service. The importance of protecting family and friends is often as important in the Chinese culture as protecting oneself and improving the stature of the Chinese community. It is considered an insult to ask people whether they have done what they said they would do.

The city team, Team Three, was composed of workers on loan from Special Services for Children (SSC). They were skilled in the procedures of this unit. In general, this skill was useful; they knew agencies and staffs and had connections with SSC and other agencies that they could use to good advantage. The primary dis-

advantage of this team was that its members had been chosen for
skills and styles of working both with clients and with agencies, but
these styles and skills did not include contracting and monitoring.
Initially, their feelings about the service model were summed up by
one worker: "I do all the work anyway, then when things are in
order I get a contract signed. I can't hold up services because a
piece of paper isn't signed."

Their attitude not only reflects the commitment to service
before all else but also recognizes the added difficulties of contracting. City team workers found it easier to get agencies involved in
doing the emergency work required than to meet with individual
agencies to plan the case by using a case-conference model of their
own making. After services began, the contract was presented as
"just another agency procedure I have to follow." The methods of
monitoring were informal and presented in a manner that implicitly
asked, "Can I help you with this case?" In the hands of a skilled
worker, this style gets the job done but avoids the difficulties of
educating agencies and staff about contracting and monitoring.
Although a great deal of skilled and difficult work was done by this
team, unlearning prior techniques and procedures was a slow
process. By 1978, a considerable, positive change toward the model
had occurred due to the perseverance of the team leader, Terry
Windward. One of her workers, Harry Sofpaint, wrote:

> The LESFU method of using contracts is a very
> useful tool, which I intend to use when I go back to
> SSC. The monitoring role of LESFU . . . represents
> another technique that I intend to take back to SSC. In
> monitoring, it is important to bring across to the other
> agency that you are not watching over them. . . . You
> are working with them to see that the client gets the
> service. For years the leaders of the private and public
> sectors have been meeting and talking about cooperation
> whereas in reality none of them has wanted it. Each
> "side" tends to want most what the "other side" has and,
> in the process of their bickering, both workers and clients
> suffer. On the private side, the multiplicity of the agen-
> cies has caused duplication of services. On the public
> side, the overall service network is well set-up on paper

but in reality, due to mismanagement, there are large pools of more adequately paid social service staff performing functions . . . to justify the existence of the bureaucratic "empire." LESFU represents a first step in bringing about more integration between the public and private sectors—a step that is long overdue.

Team One, which was predominantly Hispanic, reflected the concerns of the team leader, John Goya. He was committed to serving the needs of Hispanic people and was also the most committed, conceptually and practically, to the contract model of service. He held in mind and emphasized to his team the importance of serving in a demonstration program and of following the practices called for by the model. Goya himself worked out a general format for monitoring: The last item in the contract spelled out the details of monitoring service; a final clause of the contract, which was dated with each signature, indicated that a reconvening would be held at a specified time to evaluate the case and plan changes in service.

The Team One contracts also usually specified whose responsibility it was to communicate about a breakdown in service, thereby attempting to establish lines of accountability as well as communication. Essentially, this team utilized three different types of meetings for monitoring: setting up regular meetings, if only to inform and reemphasize group process; meeting with all agencies around specific crises or when at the beginning it is clear that a follow-up meeting is needed; and inviting only those immediately involved in a specific issue to a meeting. Although Goya had the least-experienced and least-professional staff—in terms of length of experience and previous education—it produced some of the best-conceptualized and best-written contracts.

The willingness to move up the levels of agency hierarchy to settle service monitoring and delivery problems is fraught with difficulty. For many LESFU workers to move in this direction would have damaged the only factor that they had going for themselves consistently—their friendly relations with workers in other agencies. Yet good will is often not enough to ensure competent service delivery, and a central notion of the contract approach was the ability to enforce delivery on agreements, moving away from personal good will as the determinant of service quality. LESFU's motto was "We monitor the cases, not the workers."

The reaction to monitoring seemed to be idiosyncratic— those who were comfortable with the concept and approached agencies with a cooperative strategy generally had positive and consistent feedback and replanning sessions with other agencies. Workers lacking this spirit of joint enterprise from previous experience, personal makeup, or training had much greater difficulty in monitoring contracts. Personality was decidedly an issue. Those who conveyed assertiveness, helpfulness, and concern were clearly more successful.

But monitoring techniques cannot be developed by or left up to the line workers' personalities. Too much depends on the structure, procedures, and priorities of cooperating agencies. In mid 1977, Brahms undertook a round of meetings with executives and staffs of other agencies to discuss contracting and monitoring. Only if these meetings lead to ongoing analysis and mutual development of various techniques can progress be expected in monitoring and in dealing with the impediments to better service. The difficulty lies in the patterns of relations internal to and between social agencies, and it relates to agencies' concepts of the helping process, as well as to agencies' own views of accountability. Until these issues are dealt with, LESFU will continue to depend on three techniques for contracting and monitoring: personal relationships among workers, involvement of workers with client problems, and regular reconvenings.

The current LESFU monitoring process does include a degree of enforcing accountability. In some agencies, when clients receive poor service or no service, vague report phrases, such as "client resistant to service," and "client does not respond to repeated contacts," mask the failures. The LESFU model makes service visible; workers can be questioned, team leaders can request a meeting with supervisors in other agencies to discuss client needs and contact executives of agencies, and finally repeated complaints can be made public at the LESFU board.

In the long run, the idea of one agency, such as LESFU, holding others accountable in a monitoring sense will undoubtedly have to be expanded and complemented with a more collaborative stance based on mutual accountability. This stance must emphasize ongoing clarification with clients and agencies about workers' roles, as well as continual reassessment of the clients' needs and tasks (Rhodes, 1977). To do this effectively, the staffs of cooperating agencies will have to be convinced of the value of contracting, including mutual goals and client participation. They will also need extensive training in using contracts as helping mechanisms, since each provider agency actually has a subcontract with each client. Systematic feedback of what happens to clients is an important impetus for organizational change. Ultimately, this may be monitoring's most important function.

Utility of the Model

Although more work needs to be done to develop interagency methods of accountability and techniques for service and contract monitoring, the service model was useful for engaging a variety of agencies, as noted in Table 4. To a considerable extent, it was possible to eliminate duplicating services and, as a corollary, reduce client manipulation. LESFU took responsibility for the whole family complex of problems. This aspect is critical in the model and sets LESFU apart from other agencies because accountability is a formal part of the work.

With LESFU, when children go into placement, they have advocates whose interest and incentive is to get them out of placement as quickly as possible. LESFU has a strong record in this regard. In 1977, the average placement term of seventeen of the twenty-two children placed was two months, compared to an average of five years of foster placement in New York State for those children who stay over six months in foster care. In no other agency structure within the child welfare and foster care system is there a clearly defined advocate for taking the child out of placement and providing services to assist the family in readjustment. Unless a parent engages a lawyer, generally there is no one to assist in reclaiming the child.

It is not the clear responsibility of foster care workers or the clear mandate of the SSC to get a child out as soon as it is safe and feasible. It is often talked about, but the structure does not support the SSC worker or foster care workers in efforts to reunite a family. Public money goes to foster care; workers have little time

Table 4. Agencies Providing Services to Active LESFU
High-Risk Families.

Agency	Number of Different Families Served
Special Services for Children	48
Department of Social Services	48
Bellevue Hospital	36
Board of Education	30
Gouverneur Hospital	24
Harold Street Settlement	20
Family Court	20
N. Y. C. Housing Authority	19
Beth Israel Hospital	15
Monroe House	14
Mobilization for Youth Legal Services	12
Collegiate Settlement	10
Recreational Alliance	8
Visiting Nurse Service	8
Social Security Administration	6
Agency for Child Development	6
Catholic Home Bureau	5
Chinatown Planning Council	4
MFY Inc.	4
Office of Probation	3
Sloan Center for Children	3
Manhattan Developmental Center	3
North East Neighborhood Association	3
Police	2
HIP Medical Group	2
Delancey Street Health Station	2
Retarded Infants Service	2
Brooklyn Home for Children	2
Metropolitan Hospital	2
St. Vincent's Hospital	2
Institute of Rehabilitation Medicine	2
Legal Aid Society	2
The Door	2
N.Y. Foundling Hospital	2
N.Y. Infirmary	2
Boys Club of New York	2
Other (agencies each providing service to one family)	52

to offer the natural parent and they often are left on their own to get the child back—often a monumental task involving several major bureaucracies.

Although LESFU was not overwhelmingly successful with the so-called "high-risk client," commitment to work with high-risk families was significant and different from most other agencies, where the more responsive clients get service and those "not ready" or less responsive habitually are underserved. LESFU workers feel they prevented many unnecessary placements of children. The research effort dropped this focus, but it was clear that the agency's work resulted in a good deal more success than was documented in the contracts. Clients who initially refused to accept service often called back; clients whom no one else would serve were helped. The situation was especially apparent in relation to older adolescents, who were more or less outside their parents' control and often became a primary concern of the agency. There were few services available for these adolescents and no coordinated way to work with the schools, which were not organized for the problem child. According to Penn, "If you get into trouble or get to be a problem in schools, they ignore you." In essence, there was very little to coordinate. LESFU became their central service agency.

One virtue of the model bears repetition—it allows for and necessitates more open collaboration with and accountability to the client than is mandated by many other agencies. The "illness" model of more traditional agencies sees clients as not fully able to participate in the planning of services for their family and as unable to withstand pressure or criticism from agencies or to hold other agencies accountable. Since part of the LESFU model involves helping clients learn to negotiate social welfare systems for themselves, the involvement of the client in such planning is not only appropriate but necessary. It is part of client self-determination, which social casework honors more often in the breach than in reality, because the structure of traditional service provides few opportunities for its practice.

In a series of interviews with workers in other agencies, LESFU consistently received high praise for its work from all agencies that did not see themselves as case managers. Tables 3 and 4 show that more referrals were received from such agencies. Typical comments included: "I'm relieved when I have a client in LESFU's area, I know they'll get service"; "They really extend themselves"; "No one else is willing to go in and out of clients' homes"; and "They help."

By early 1978, the team leaders and Brahms agreed that the

staff had gained and built a solid understanding of the model of work. As Brahms noted, "Even if they don't always do it according to the model, they know what the model is and can describe it." A process of internalization had taken place with a staff that initially had not had full understanding of or agreement with the style of work called for by the LESFU model. The amount of time necessary to operationalize the model had been grossly underestimated. In many ways, the agency was just arriving at the point where it could fully mount its demonstration three to four years after it had begun operation.

8

Issues, Problems, and Principles of Designing Social Programs

As a representative of a funding source, Judith Ash hoped the LESFU project would answer the question: "Should a fully developed program plan and design be required before funding agencies consider service integration or any other program proposal?" Applicants such as LESFU often argue that they need funds to develop and refine the specific techniques and procedures they will be using. This chapter provides the answer suggested by the LESFU demonstration.

Theory of Design

Although program plans cannot always be completely spelled out, the manner in which they will be operationalized should be stated. Are the designers operating on a contingency view of

121

design? In this view, they work like architects planning a house. Using deductive logic, the program designer selects structures, procedures, and subsystems compatible with the external environment, strategy, task, staff skills, top management style, and existing culture (Lorsch, 1977). Another theory of design suggests that the contingency model requires too much rationality and knowledge. Weick (1977) suggests that a self-designing system is more appropriate: "The most elementary level of self-design involves generating alternatives and testing them against the requirements and constraints perceived by people in the organization. Discrediting the hard-won lessons of experience may seem silly in generating designs. However, we have to remember that the lessons from experience are always dated. The world in which they are learned changes chronically and discontinuously. The key factor in this design system is the distribution of information and its dissemination to all parts of the organization so adaptations may take place" (Pfeffer and Salancik, 1977, p. 24). Induction rather than deduction takes precedence. Although there is much to debate about the various approaches, funding sources should insist that planners spell out their design position whether fixed, contingency, or self-design and explain how they expect to operationalize it.

LESFU mixed the self-design and contingency views. The contracting, monitoring and interorganizational relationships were to be worked out in practice, but not until January 1978 did the agency, with the help of a consultant, develop a tracking system of the problems, barriers to service, and responses of clients to service.

The problems which LESFU clients face can be grouped into ten areas: public assistance, housing, employment, parenting, child behavior, debt and money management, child health, adult health, placement, and other problems. Barriers, practical complications that keep clients from getting needed services, can make it difficult for SWAs to obtain work agreements and goal statements but are a bigger problem when it is time to arrange services through convening and contracting. The most frequently encountered barriers at LESFU are:

1. Provider not available: A worker cannot locate any agency in the community that provides the service a client needs. For example, a

worker might not be able to find an agency providing in-home training for retarded children.

2. Payment or eligibility problem: Clients cannot get the service needed because they cannot afford it (payment problem), or because the family is not eligible for the service (for example, daycare) or payment for it (for example, not eligible for Medicaid for child health care).
3. Language problem: Clients cannot get necessary services because they cannot communicate with providers.
4. Transportation: No means to reach a service for either LESFU or clients.
5. Child care: Clients cannot keep service appointments because they must stay at home to watch their children.
6. Other: An other code is provided on LESFU records to deal with reporting any other barriers that occur.

Obviously, LESFU social work associates are as dependent on clients to follow the LESFU model as clients are on LESFU. Getting clients to cooperate with LESFU is a clients' response issue. LESFU's goal is more ambitious than simply having clients cooperate. More important is helping clients learn how to address their Getting clients to cooperate with LESFU is a client response issue. also include situations or difficulties in which clients are not able to deal with their own problems. These issues are:

1. Not recognizing problems: Clients refuse to face a problem that obviously exists in the family. For example, a parent refuses to admit to a drug or alcohol problem or to neglect of children, preventing a work agreement.
2. Not taking action: Clients admit that a problem exists, for example, children have not had shots, but appear unwilling or unable to deal with the problem. For example, the father of a family may refuse to spend money on doctor bills, precluding a work agreement, goals, or client follow-through on a contract.
3. Not able to negotiate with providers: Clients are unable to effectively advocate for themselves with providers. For example, a woman may not be able to force a welfare worker to explain why her check has been reduced or to get a replacement for a stolen check.
4. Not keeping appointments: Clients fail to remember or to go to

scheduled appointments with providers, for example, hospital appointments for child health care.

5. Not following service plan: Clients do not follow the contract or plan of service (if a contract is not yet established) for reasons other than not keeping appointments. For example, a client fails to follow diets or medications ordered by the doctor.

6. Other: A code for client response issues not included in the preceding points.

If the service barriers are removed and the client is responding correctly, LESFU's efforts to follow its model may still be frustrated by providers. Providers can be troublesome by not reacting appropriately to client needs and by not following LESFU's contract and monitoring efforts. The provider issues that often arise for LESFU are:

1. Service not available: The provider, a daycare center for example, that should serve clients simply does not have room or time for the clients.

2. Refusal to serve client: The provider will not provide an available service. For example, a provider refuses to help a client because the agency feels the client is "difficult."

3. Not providing required services: The service given by the provider is not the one the client needs. For example, a school places a retarded client in a regular classroom instead of in a special education class.

4. Poor quality service: There is a fine line between the last point and this one. Here the *type* of service appears to be correct for clients but the quality of it is poor. For example, a child is receiving good child care at a Medicaid center but the provider is not explaining treatment and medications to the mother.

5. Resisting contracting: The provider refuses to give information on a case under contract to LESFU, or it resists LESFU associates' monitoring efforts in other ways.

6. Other: An other code is provided for provider response issues that do not fit under other categories.

No doubt this tracking system will help LESFU refine and improve its efforts. The categories are straightforward and could be constructed by any reasonably experienced child welfare researcher.

Had the funding sources insisted in 1974 that contingency plans include a description of the agency's techniques for revealing operational problems, a good approximation of this system could certainly have been made then. LESFU would have benefited from such a demand. Funding sources should insist on seeing how a program's intelligence system will operate prior to funding. Funding sources may want a program to have enough flexibility to develop, but they may realize it has problems once it is in operation. The best way out of this dilemma is to insist prior to funding that agencies have well-developed procedures and mechanisms for dealing with operating problems.

The fact that ultimately the agency developed such a system illustrates LESFU's capacity to adapt and change. When the state lost interest in researching placement prevention, the agency developed a management information system that would provide answers to questions about the effectiveness of the service model as well as data on how to alter present policies and procedures to improve effectiveness. Few agencies have done as much. The challenge for LESFU and other agencies that develop information systems is to deal effectively with the organizational tensions such systems uncover. Creating an open communication system that encourages recognizing and sharing tensions is an important first step.

Program Theory

Another demand that funding sources should make relates to the theory from which a project is derived. LESFU was funded on the basis that it was designed to deal with an important and real problem, a necessary but not sufficient reason for funding a project. A program related to interorganizational cooperation should rest on some theory of organizational relations.

People who write about coordination tend to be either extremely pessimistic or extremely optimistic. The latter continue to promote the idea of coordination as the preferred method of providing greater rationality in the delivery of services: improved communication, joint planning, and coordinated program operations—the interorganizational approach.

Pressman and Wildavsky (1973, pp. 133–135) are perhaps

the most articulate of the pessimists: "No phrase expresses as frequent a complaint about the federal government as does 'lack of coordination.' No suggestion for reform is more common than 'What we need is more coordination.' The word *coordination* has a deceptively simple appearance . . . Participants in a common enterprise may act in a contradictory fashion because of ignorance; when informed of their place in the scheme of things, they may be expected to behave obediently. If we relax the assumption that a common purpose is involved, however, and admit the possibility (indeed the likelihood) of conflict over goals, then *coordination* becomes another term for *coercion*. Coordination thus becomes a form of power. Achieving coordination . . . means getting your own way. You can't learn how to do it from a slogan."

Some theoreticians concerned with coordination of services deal with the issue of optimal conditions for predicting successful coordination. Reid (1964) suggests the goal-related exchange of resources—personnel, services, facilities, information, funds, and clients—as key factors in organizational cooperation. According to Reid, for coordination to take place there must be shared goals, complementary resources, efficient mechanisms for patrolling coordination, and cost benefits. He notes that coordination may not only be too difficult but also too expensive from an agency's point of view.

Sebring (1977) suggests that there are many sources of interorganizational uncooperativeness: past unsuccessful encounters among personnel; misunderstandings about each other's environmental pressures and constraints; and different organizational goals, reward structures, and time orientations. Other factors include managerial style, constraints of operating procedures, separation among the cooperating groups, gripes about professionals and organizations, formal rules, control procedures, and the hierarchy of reporting. Any of these formulations, among many others, would have helped LESFU anticipate problems with certain types of organizations. Instead, it approached each agency without any real foreknowledge of what to expect.

Monitoring and contracting were keys to LESFU's service model. There was a desperate need over the years for a theory that might illuminate these processes. Davidson (1976) has suggested a three-stage planning framework to assist in making informed decisions about appropriate interorganizational undertakings. Three sets of issues must be examined: environmental pressures, such as the state of the economy, and pressures from various groups and interests related to an agency; organizational characteristics, such as resources and domain; and the interorganizational planning process.

Interorganizational relations, such as contract convenings, involve group interaction of individuals. Groups go through phases, such as an exploratory phase, in which the participants feel each other out; a task definition phase, in which they decide whether or not to face the real problems of cooperative work; and a working together phase, in which they actually tackle problems. The concept of a group's history or life cycle adds another dynamic factor, time, to the analysis of interorganizational relations.

The fact that individual members of a coordinating group occupy at least two roles—one in the coordinating group and one in their own organization—that are in conflict sometimes, influences the group's ability to accomplish explicit goals. These mixed motives are complicated because while relations among organizations are being considered at one level, at another level, they are interpersonal relations. After all, individuals span the boundaries between the organizations and make the decisions regarding the extent and nature of the cooperation (Davidson, 1976).

To lessen conflict and improve attitudes toward coordination, several types of consensus among involved individuals are required (Benson and others, 1973). These include domain consensus, ideological consensus, and interorganizational evaluation consensus, in which workers in one organization judge work in another organization. In this complex situation, the absence or presence of skillful leadership is a crucial factor in creating consensus. Strong leadership cannot eliminate any of the phases that a coordinating group must experience, but it may reduce their length and smooth the transitions. Leadership also cannot overcome conditions in an organization's structure and environment that work against cooperation.

LESFU could certainly have used such ideas for understanding why some agencies seemed trustful and others mistrustful of the service model. Funders should have insisted that LESFU be grounded in organizational theory. Staff and management are constantly in need of explanations as to why some ideas and activities work well and others fail. When theory is not available, the mass of data, attitudes, and feelings can present a quite confusing picture.

Unfortunately there is a lack of useful practice theory. When planners fall back on evidence from past experiences, these sources should be carefully scrutinized by funding sources. LESFU did not completely digest the experiences of the 1960s' poverty program, as its activities in relation to paraprofessionals, ethnicity, boards of directors, and community organizing attest.

Dilemmas of Design

Although it is unrealistic to expect program designers to anticipate all of the problems that may crop up in programs, they could be required to estimate the difficulty expected in implementation. On the basis of the LESFU experience, it is possible to delineate certain general design problems. These concerns can be grouped under the headings of staff, clients, board, goals, procedures, and resources. Problems of implementation are, at the core, problems of constraints. To achieve one end, another end may be jeopardized. How to steer a course between the constraints is the problem for management. In hindsight, had the following questions been put to the designers of LESFU, their design would have been tighter or, at the least, they might have phased in the project differently and altered the sequence in which various problems were faced.

Staff. Are you constructing jobs that people will want to do? Are you constructing jobs that are workable? Will your staff possess certain characteristics that may deflect them from carrying out their assignments in the prescribed manner? What ongoing tensions will the staff have to deal with? What rewards and supports have you built in for the staff? How much training of the staff will be required?

Clients. What attitudes and skills must clients possess to fit into your program? What assumptions are you making about the clients? If clients fail to live up to your assumptions, where will problems arise first in the program? Do you have any procedures for adjusting to client preferences?

Board. How will the board keep abreast of what is happening in a program? What interests should be represented on the board? What adjustments in board procedure will have to be made if the staff participates at board meetings?

Goals. What conflicts exist among your goals? What uncontrollable resources do you need to achieve your goals? Are your goals measurable? What are the indexes of goal attainment?

Procedures. Which parts of your service procedure are potentially in conflict? Which are dependent on the completion of other parts? Which of your procedures are not operationalized? How much time have you estimated for operationalizing various aspects of the program? Are any of your procedures ideologically rooted? How will you recognize unforeseen contingencies before they create goal displacements? How will you keep dysfunctional informal procedures from being implemented?

Resources. Do you have sufficient sanction to achieve your goals? What problems will your funding arrangements cause? Are there gaps in knowledge of practice related to any aspect of the program? If research is contemplated, what strains may emerge with service staff?

In answering these questions, program designers must recognize that their responses can never be final. Most of the questions represent dilemmas—for example, all goals conflict to some extent, few workers want to do everything required, and there are usually gaps in knowledge. As such, the tension aroused by the nature of the dilemmas will have to be managed. LESFU evolved a communication system that kept many tensions from being hidden or deflected into negative or dysfunctional activities. Combined with the tracking or accountability system, it channeled frustration and disagreement into concern for organizational improvements. Effective organizations require such systems.

Perhaps these questions were not asked because the funding sources were primarily interested in the question, "Can unstable families in inner-city neighborhoods be helped?" Partly because the questions were not addressed, the best answer that LESFU can provide at this point in its history is that some families can be permanently helped and many others can be given needed assistance in times of crisis. Although the service model does not guarantee family growth and development, it vigorously promotes such advancement. Accessibility is dramatically improved, the chances of continuity of service increase, client redress becomes an operational reality, and accountability is organizationally anchored.

Systematic research will provide much sharper answers and evidence. Nevertheless, the LESFU experience does corroborate the findings of other research projects. In a controlled experiment related to work with natural parents of children in placement, Stein and Gambrill (1977, p. 507) note that "The probabilities of parents' following through with planning and having their children returned were significantly greater when a contract was signed than when it was not." (Behavioral modification techniques were used in both the control and experimental groups.)

It is likely that the contract model is a useful method for child welfare projects, although Stein and Gambrill's experiment and the LESFU experience do not answer the question of which theory of helping is more effective—brief services, task-orientation, behavior modification, or an ecological or ego-psychological approach. "Of those clients who signed contracts, the response, while hesitant at first, was overwhelmingly positive. Clients often remarked that the content of the contracts was the first specific information they had received indicating precisely what had to be done in order to work toward having a child returned to their care and that having a copy of the contract at home provided a ready reference point for regular 'checks' as to what was expected on a daily or weekly basis. The specificity, as well as the minimum conditions set forth for restoration of a child, were very positively received by members of the bench, particularly in instances where termination of parental rights were pursued" (1977, p. 502).

The best answer to which method of helping should be used along with contracting is that most clients go through a series of stages during treatment and, to some extent, these stages dictate what services can most effectively be offered to the client. Initially, and for some time after intake and diagnosis, clients are probably in their most resistant phase. Support and advocacy services are most successful at this stage since the client is not likely to be ready to accept more therapeutic services. Concrete actions on the part of the service provider, such as help in finding new housing or a daycare center, go a long way toward improving the client's life and developing the client's responsiveness to other services. Once the client is interested in a program, therapeutically or educationally oriented services—either individually or in groups—are appropriate. During this receptive phase, the client should be prepared for the final phase and the termination of treatment (Berkeley Planning Associates, 1976).

Nevertheless, Rhodes' (1977, p. 139) conclusion should be borne in mind by those interested in contracting: "The concept of contract negotiation, which has achieved widespread support from various theoretical models of social work practice, has not been developed with any systematic rigor." Certainly the same can be said for LESFU's multiagency contracts, which, if anything, were much more complex than the worker-client contracts that the research referred to earlier relates to.

Another issue for those who would replicate LESFU relates to the necessity of creating integrating agencies. Could a social worker employed by and operating out of a school use LESFU's service model? Could each settlement house have case managers on its staff? Or should the family court organize its social work department into a LESFU-like operation? Although the existing service situation in any particular locality and its constraints will often be deciding factors, there are general concerns to consider. Case managers in host settings, such as schools, will probably have to face a series of pressures emanating from the host settings' major concerns. For example, in schools the major concern is to educate children, not to solve their emotional and social problems. Could the schools maintain a family focus, orienting themselves to adult members of a child's family?

Making LESFU one unit of a larger service organization, such as a department of social services or a settlement house, would create profound changes and strains in such organizations. Where this has been attempted, tensions have developed because service specialists feared that service managers would constantly monitor their work; service managers feared regulation and relegation to clerical functions and wished to provide services themselves. Staff members isolated themselves into their own staff units and became highly protective of their domain (Rosenberg and Brody, 1974).

Serious dilemmas of organizational change will have to be dealt with when case managers are introduced into existing service organizations.

The Team Three city workers saw LESFU as a great improvement on the present organization of the Department of Social Services. One worker from the department's Special Services for Children (SSC) division observed:

> The most immediate difference between working at SSC and the Family Union is simply one of location . . . Covering a whole borough from one central location, as is done presently at SSC, means that you can see far fewer clients in a given day and also spend less time going into people's problems and helping to solve them, once you do get to the home . . . Being in the same neighborhood gives the worker a chance to get to know the different agencies and . . . to help the clients make more meaningful contacts because you know first-hand which people and agencies can be of the most help. Also, being in the neighborhood and being seen every day means that a more trusting relationship is built up between the worker and the people who live there. . . . If caseworkers are sent out to work with people and agencies in a given neighborhood, there is more of an incentive to do a good job. There is no big mysterious bureaucracy to hide behind—everyone knows what you are doing and, if someone wants to see you, you are easy to find.
>
> The two main field operations of SSC are Protective Services and Family Services. When a protective worker finishes investigating a case, he may feel that there is no ongoing abuse or neglect but that the family may need ongoing help. He may . . . refer the case to the Family Services section, which in theory is supposed to work something like LESFU and hopefully will be set up like LESFU as we demonstrate that placement of children can be prevented by [such] an agency. At the present time, Family Services workers have a difficult time doing preventive work because they get cases all over the borough and . . . court supervision cases that

> used to be handled by the probation department. . . .
> Many of the court cases could have been kept out of
> the crisis court stage if the family could have had access
> to help nearby.

The suggestion to locate LESFU in the family court raises the issue of whether public agencies can cooperate with one another. In child welfare, public agencies have seldom been effective monitors of private agencies. Yet Wilson and Rachal (1977) point out that in general it is easier for a public agency to change the behavior of a private organization than that of another public agency. Private organizations can be sued or enjoined in court by a public agency; it is extremely rare for one public agency to sue another. The courts cannot and will not mediate internal disputes among executive agencies or require one agency to do something that it has the legal authority to refuse; nor can the courts tell an agency that it must use its legitimate discretionary authority to act as another agency would prefer.

Wilson and Rachal dispute the idea that by giving elected officials authority over subordinate agencies and grouping agencies in sufficiently rational categories, the government will be effective and accountable. They feel that "no acceptable level of authority or feasible organizational scheme can produce coherently consistent policies given congressional and other sources of intervention and given administrative apparatus of a certain size . . . Large scale public enterprise and widespread public regulation may be incompatible" (Wilson and Rachal, 1977, p. 14). If this is the case, public service agencies need a complement of private service deliverers. The public services might be organized like LESFU, coordinating the services of private providers. Perhaps the past weakness of public monitoring of private services was related to the absence of locally based public case managers.

Whatever mix of public and private is made, the city workers were affected by their LESFU experience and played an important role in the agency. The LESFU teams were constantly calling the city team with questions of how to deal with family courts, child welfare, and other systems; they also asked about potentially useful contacts. The city team frequently called the neighborhood workers about what agency to deal with, how the neighborhood system works, and how to handle particular ethnic problems; they also asked for local references. Cross fertilization strengthened the agency. Perhaps this points to the need for both public and private service managers and service providers.

Similarly, the sentiments leading to cooperation among staffs of different agencies take considerable time and experience to develop. Agencies and professional groups with long histories of independence can be expected in most cases to resist the establishment of a central authority for program integration, which would control funds and assignments of responsibility (Redburn, 1975). LESFU-like service integration projects, of a much more limited intention, may be a necessary stage prior to comprehensive integration of programs. As Beck (1978, pp. 30–32) notes:

An important aspect of the union's invention of the contract with the agencies went to the problem of autonomy and sovereignty. Since agencies tend to seek their own survival and their own aggrandizement, integration efforts that look toward the merger of these different interests are likely to fail. Even if they are successful, there can be a loss of desirable pluralism and creativity. The union, however, only asks that autonomy and sovereignty be given up in respect to particular family situations. The threat to agency survival is minimal.

The contract provisions of the Lower East Side Family Union pointed the way in which services might be integrated within a county or within an urban district without interfering with the categorical approach to problem solving that is inherent in the operation of Congress and lies at the root of the problem posed by fractionated human services in the local community. The union idea essentially says that money can flow from federal government to state government to city government to neighborhood and that it can have all the strings attached to it that are inherent in the regulatory model but that it is possible to create a device in a local area which forces all deliverers to work together around particular families.

There is now . . . increasing interest in development of the local government, and this is manifest in

Title XX of the Social Security Act, which provides a kind of bloc grant in the social services. Title XX mandates local planning . . . As part of that planning, there could be created in counties and urban districts a public presence, which would essentially demand that all agencies which received public funds participate in a LESFU-like arrangement as a condition of securing such funds.

The LESFU experience reveals certain limitations of service integration projects. Such projects in and of themselves do not expand the types of services available. Often it is the lack of employment or housing that is crucial to a family's stability; LESFU intends where possible to use its community organization team to agitate for additional resources, as well as to organize volunteer services. Service integration projects can become flooded with requests for service; this leads to restraint in outreach or publicizing services. In such situations the more articulate are more likely to be served.

No case record, case management, or information system at the local level can completely correct or undo program fragmentation at the city, state, or federal level. Case management is not a panacea (Kahn, 1976). Without clear objectives or behavioral outcomes, it is difficult to tell if case coordination is an improvement over the prior service delivery system. Within reasonable limits, conflict and competition are not wholly undesirable. Different groups see problems in different ways and have various contributions to make toward their solution. Neglected areas of social services have been those for which nobody fought (Brown, 1975). The idea of service manager generalists and service provider specialists could lead to new problems of overspecialization and fragmentation. In addition, not everyone who seeks help has the ability or desire to enter into the process of setting goals and developing service agreements (Rosenberg and Brody, 1974).

Summary

The LESFU experience leaves a number of questions about the costs of service integration. As Gilbert and Specht (1977) ask, at what point does the cost of coordinating a large number of organizations outweigh the benefits? Given the dynamics of increasing demand for varieties and quality of services with increasing costs, should social provisions or social services be given priority?

Bernard (1975) observes that social services that aim to change people's behavior, attitudes, or values are not substitutes for social reform nor are they cures for social problems. Social provisions that aim at providing resources for a defined level of well-being, for example, guaranteed income and public housing, are also not good devices for quickly solving social problems such as crime, delinquency, and alcoholism nor will they quickly change the values, attitudes, and skills of people. Adequate social services and social provisions are necessary for a humane civilization. However, there is no single strategy or program that can or should preempt all other social efforts (Bernard, 1975). Education, religion, politics, and economic programs are all important. Social programs that combine provisions and services have an important part to play in the resolution of social problems. As programs, such as LESFU, refine themselves, they help to redefine and clarify the nature of social problems as well as their role in solving the problems. LESFU was able to redefine its view of unnecessary placement. At the same time, the agency saw that it could not systematically focus on a social problem, by understanding the part it could play in resolving the problem, until it had improved its techniques. Fortunately, LESFU developed a structure open enough to make redefinition and refinement possible. The accountability and communication systems working in tandem were the key to this structure.

Social services programs now primarily help a subgroup among a target population that believes a service fits their needs and is delivered in an acceptable manner. Two appropriate questions are: How can the excluded be helped? And, can services be reshaped to be effective for those left out? The funders of LESFU can be assured that their money was used to answer these questions; services were indeed shaped in ways that widened their net of acceptability and increased their range of effectiveness.

Further experimentation and research will no doubt more fully clarify the utility of LESFU's approach. Program designers can learn a great deal from the way the project developed. Perhaps the most important lesson is how to approach their job. "Proponents from the public arena stress lowering costs, coordinating services, minimizing red tape, and maximizing the impact of all the scarce (and continually shrinking) resources. Social work proponents focus on reducing the number of out-of-home placements, improving the ability of families to function, reducing the dependency of people, and ensuring appropriate care for children. From a client's point of view, the system must be made easier to enter and understand, as well as open to participation in decision making." This is what they all want. Individually, they do not say or often know what they will do if there is insufficient money, knowledge, sanction, or support. What they can get should be the major concern of program designers, whose skills should include the ability to construct communication and accountability systems that make participants aware of the pressure each one operates under.

References

BECK, B. M. "Community Control: A Distraction, Not an Answer." *Social Work*, 1969, *14*, 14–20.

BECK, B. M. *The Lower East Side Family Union: A Social Invention*. New York: Foundation for Child Development, 1978.

BENSON, J. K., and OTHERS. "Coordinating Human Services: A Sociological Study of an Interorganizational Network." Washington, D.C.: Project Share, 1973. (Mimeograph.)

Berkeley Planning Associates. *Planning and Implementing Child Abuse and Neglect Service Programs*. Washington, D.C.: Berkeley Planning Associates, 1976.

BERNARD, S. "Why Service Delivery Programs Fail." *Social Work*, 1975, *20*, 206–210.

BROWN, R. G. S. *The Management of Welfare*. London: Martin Robertson, 1975.

BUSH, S. "A Family-Help Program That Really Works." *Psychology Today,* 1977, *11,* 49–50, 84, 88.

Citizens' Committee for Children. *A Dream Deferred.* New York: Citizens' Committee for Children, 1971.

Citizens' Committee for Children. *A Dream Still Deferred.* New York: Citizens' Committee for Children, 1975.

Council of State Governments. *Human Services Integration: State Functions in Implementation.* Lexington, Ky.: Council of State Governments, 1974.

DAVIDSON, S. M. "Planning and Coordination of Social Services in Multiorganizational Contexts." *Social Service Review,* 1976, *50,* 117–137.

ENARSON, H. "The Art of Planning, or Watching You Get It All Together." *New York Times,* October 4, 1975, p. 27.

GAGE, R. W. "Integration of Human Services Delivery Systems." *Public Welfare,* 1976, *58,* 27–33.

GILBERT, N., and SPECHT, H. *Dimensions of Social Welfare Policy.* Englewood Cliffs, N.J.: Prentice-Hall, 1974.

GILBERT, N., and SPECHT, H. "Quantitative Aspects of Social Service Coordination Efforts: Is More Better?" *Administration in Social Work,* 1977, *1,* 53–61.

HARGROVE, E. *The Missing Link.* Washington, D.C.: Urban Institute, 1975.

HEIFETZ, H. "Introduction." In H. H. Weissman (Ed.), *Community Development in the Mobilization for Youth Experience.* New York: Association Press, 1969.

JONES, H. "The Use of Indigenous Personnel as Service Givers." In H. H. Weissman (Ed.), *Individual and Group Services in the Mobilization For Youth Experience.* New York: Association Press, 1969.

KADUSHIN, A. *Child Welfare Services.* New York: Macmillan, 1974.

KAHN, A. J. *Theory and Practice of Social Planning.* New York: Russell Sage Foundation, 1969.

KAHN, A. J. "Service Delivery at the Neighborhood Level: Experience, Theory, and Fads." *Social Service Review,* 1976, *50,* 23–56.

KELTY, E. J. "Is Services Integration Dangerous to Your Mental Health?" *Evaluation,* 1976, *3,* 139–141, 159.

LORSCH, J. W. "Organization Design: A Situational Perspective." *Organizational Dynamics,* 1977, *6,* 2–14.

MALLUCCIO, A. N., and MARLOW, W. D. "The Case for the Contract." *Social Work,* 1974, *19,* 28–36.

"A Managerial Model for Child Welfare Decision Making." Unpublished grant proposal submitted to Research Review Panel, Office of Child Development, Department of Health, Education, and Welfare, 1976.

MAYER, J., and TIMMS, N. *The Client Speaks.* New York: Atherton, 1970.

MELD, M. "Human Service Integration: Toward a Humanistic Approach." In *The Social Welfare Forum, 1976.* New York: Columbia University Press, 1977.

MIDDLEMAN, R., and GOLDBERG, G. *Social Service Delivery: A Structural Approach to Social Work Practice.* New York: Columbia University Press, 1974.

PERROW, C. "The Bureaucratic Paradox: The Efficient Organization Centralizes in Order to Decentralize." *Organizational Dynamics,* 1977, *4,* 3–14.

PFEFFER, J., and SALANCIK, G. R. "The Case for a Coalitional Model of Organizations." *Organizational Dynamics,* 1977, *6,* 15–29.

PRESSMAN, J., and WILDAVSKY, A. *Implementation.* Berkeley: University of California Press, 1973.

REDBURN, S. "Two Approaches to Human Services Integration." Washington, D.C.: Project Share, 1975. (Mimeograph.)

REID, W. "Interagency Coordination in Delinquency Prevention and Control." *Social Service Review,* 1964, *38,* 418–428.

RHODES, S. L. "Contract Negotiation in the Initial Stage of Casework Service." *Social Service Review,* 1977, *51,* 125–140.

RITTEL, H., and WEBBER, M. "Dilemmas in a General Theory of Planning." In N. Gilbert and H. Specht (Eds.), *Planning for Social Welfare.* Englewood Cliffs, N.J.: Prentice-Hall, 1977.

ROSENBERG, M. L., and BRODY, R. "The Threat or Challenge of Accountability." *Social Work,* 1974, *19,* 344–350.

SAHLEIN, W. J. *A Neighborhood Solution to the Social Services Dilemma.* Lexington, Mass.: Heath, 1973.

SCHUMAN, K. "Lower East Side Family Union." In J. Weintraub (Ed.), *Symposium on Status Offenders. Manual for Action.* New York: National Council of Jewish Women, 1976.

SEBRING, R. H. "An Organization-Environment Perspective on State Government-University Interorganizational Conflicts: The Case of the $5 Million Misunderstanding." Paper presented at 24th annual meeting of the Council on Social Work Education, Phoenix, Ariz., March 1977.

SELZNICK, P. *TVA and the Grass Roots.* Berkeley: University of California Press, 1949.

SPECK, R. V. "Psychotherapy of the Social Network of a Schizophrenic Family." *Family Process,* 1967, *7,* 208–214.

SPECK, R. V., and REUVENI, V. "Network Therapy—A Developing Concept." *Family Process,* 1969, *8,* 182–190.

STEIN, T. J., and GAMBRILL, E. D. "Facilitating Decision Making in Foster Care: The Alameda Project." *Social Service Review,* 1977, *51,* 502–513.

U.S. Department of Health, Education, and Welfare. "Services Integration—Next Steps." (Memorandum for the President transmitted by Secretary Elliot Richardson.) June 1, 1971a.

U.S. Department of Health, Education, and Welfare. "A Proposed Study for HEW Services Reform." Part 1. (Attachment to the June memorandum for the President transmitted by Secretary Elliot Richardson, December 23, 1971b, pp. 2–6.)

WEICK, K. E. "Organizational Design: Organizations as Self-Designing Systems." *Organizational Dynamics,* 1977, *6,* 31–46.

WEISSMAN, H. H. "Overview of the Community Development Program." In H. H. Weissman (Ed.), *Community Development in the Mobilization for Youth Experience.* New York: Association Press, 1969.

WEISSMAN, H. H. *Community Councils and Community Control.* Pittsburgh: University of Pittsburgh Press, 1970.

WILSON, J. Q., and RACHAL, P. "Can the Government Regulate Itself?" *The Public Interest,* 1977, 3–14.

Index

A

Accountability: and board's information sources, 53; and forms, development of, 84–88; and monitoring, 116; open communication system and, 94; policy formulation and, 30; structure and, 136

Administrator, role of, 38–41

Advocates, parents as, 8, 9

Agency contracts: integration of services by, 8; planning stage and, 31; report on, 71–73

Alcoholism, 13

Alms houses, 2

Antipoverty program of 1960s, 28–36, 128

Appointments, failure to keep, 123, 124

ASH, J., xii; and criticisms of LESFU,

90; and funding and program design, 212; and governor's task force on social services, 27; hiring of, 23, 24

Average term of placement, 117

B

Barriers to service, 123, 124

BECK, B. M., xii, 32, 139. *See also* Rue, H.

Behavior modification, 130

BENSON, J. K., 127, 139

BERK, J., 70

Berkeley Planning Associates, 131, 139

BERNARD, S., 136, 139

Black teams, 9, 32

Board of LESFU: and community representatives, 32; 43–45; and

143

design problems, 129; first meeting of, 43; function of, 90; and sources of information, 52; and team leaders, 70–78

BRACE, C. L., 2

BRAHMS, xiii; and accountability, 84, 86, 87; and authority system, 92; and dealing with agencies, 104, 105; and family service contracts, 66, 71, 102; and funding, 80; hiring of, 53; and monitoring, 116; and service model, 55–79, 119, 120; and staff problems, 75; and structural problems, 80–94; and team integration, 60

BRODY, R., 131, 135, 141

BROWN, R. G. S., 90, 135, 139

BURTWELL, C., 3

BUSH, S., 20, 140

C

Capacity building, 7

CARDINAL, H., 32, 70

CAREY, H., 27

Cases: and accountability, 31; management of, 135; and tracking system, 84, 92

Charities, 4

Charts. See Tables

Child care and failure to keep appointments, 123

Children's Aid Society, 2

Chinese teams, 9, 32, 113

Citizens' Committee for Children (CCC), ix, 3, 14–19, 140

Clients: and design problems, 128; and involvement in planning, 20; phases of, 130. See also High-risk families

Closing of case, 69, 70

Communication system, 92, 94, 125, 136

Community consciousness, 8

Community Mental Health Act, 5

Community organization department, 33, 34

Community organizer, 75, 87

Community participation, 29

Community residents, 40, 43, 44

Confidentiality, 104, 105, 113

Consensus among involved individuals, 127

Consolidation of agencies, 4, 5

Consultants, hiring of, 38–41, 44, 45, 83

Contingency model, 122

Contracts. See Agency contracts; Family service contracts

Cook's Tour model, 12

Coordinating services between departments, 107

Coordination of agencies, 4, 5, 21, 125–128

Cost effectiveness, 30

Costs of services, 6, 35, 95, 96, 135

Council of State Governments, 7

Counseling programs, 29

Courts, use of, 133

Crime, 13, 29, 30

D

DAVIDSON, S. M., 126, 127, 140

Debts and money management, 122

Definition of problem, 13–19

Denying services, 110

Departmental organization, 33, 34

Design of program, 28–34, 121–137

Development of model, 55–79

Dream Deferred, A, 3, 14–19, 23

Drug addiction, 13

Duplication of services, 30, 31

E

Ecological approach to social work practice, 8

Elected officials, 133

Eligibility for service, 29, 30, 123

Emotional fatigue of workers, 66

Employment problems, 13, 122

ENARSON, H., 12, 140

Ends, means versus, 37–54

Engagement, 65–67, 98–100

Essential project elements, 38

Ethnic backgrounds: of clients, 108;

and monitoring, 113; of teams, 9, 32, 60, 61
Executive director, hiring of, 52, 53
Expectations of workers, 86, 87

F

Family break-up, causes of, 19
Family service contracts, 31, 67–70; client's view of, 109–111; defined, 67; and engagement of clients, 66; form of, 88–90; and high-risk families, 75, 76; opposition to, 57; and performance, 101–104; signatures on, 108; use of, 68, 130, 131; writing of, 69. *See also* Monitoring
Family social workers, 15, 16
FIELD, B., xiii, 87
FIRESTONE, S., 47
Follow-up and monitoring, 112
Formal system, development of, 57–61
Formulation of policy, 23–36
Foster care, 2; average stay in, 117; cost to place child in, 95, 96
Foundation for Child Development grant, xii, 24, 26
Funding: permanence and, 76, 77; planning period, 25–28, 35; for prevention, 80; and program design, 121, 125; research and, 49; staffing and, 41

G

GAGE, R. W., 7, 11, 140
GAMBRILL, E. D., 130, 142
Geographical limitations, 49, 50, 57
GILBERT, N., 9, 10, 23, 35, 135, 140
Goal attainment scale, 47, 65, 100, 101
Goals, 10, 11, 47; and design problems, 129
GOLD, S.: and defense of prevention, 48; and first board meeting, 43; hiring of, 24; personality conflicts and, 52, 55, 56; responsibilities of, 30; and team integration, 60, 61;

title of, 39; and training sessions, 94
GOLDBERG, G., 103, 104, 141
Good government movement, 4
GOYA, J., xiii, 70, 115
GREENSTREET, E., 26, 31, 48, 70

H

HARGROVE, E., xi, 140
Harold Street Settlement, 13, 105
Health problems, 122
HEIFETZ, H., 13, 140
High-risk families, 49, 57, 65; commitment to, 118, 119; and contract commitment, 75, 76; definition of, 79; designation of, 86; index of, 49, 50; and outreach, 97; problems of, 122, 123; response issues and, 123, 124; table of case status report on, 85; table of sources of, 96
Hiring process, 39
Homemakers, 40, 43, 56, 99, 100
Housekeepers, 9, 40
Housing problems, 122
Human Resources Administrations, 7

I

Ideology, 43–47
Implementation of service model, xi, 96–117
Indenture, 2
Independence, teaching of, 110
Indexes of high risk, 49, 50
Indigenous workers, hiring of, 33, 35
Infanticide, 2
Informal system, 57–61
Instigators, 12–22
Integration of services, 6, 7, 134, 135
Integration of team members, 60, 61
Interorganization relations, 127
Involvement of client, 119

J

Jefferson House, 70
Job training. *See* Training
JONES, H., 40, 140

K

KADUSHIN, A., 2, 3, 140
KAHN, A. J., 4, 5, 11, 135, 140
KELTY, E. J., 6, 140

L

Language problems, 60, 61, 123
LASH, T. *See* Ash, J.
Legal aid associations, 104–106
Lewis and Clark model, 12, 13
LIVINGSTON, D., 50, 79
Local residents, 56–60
Long-term care cases, 75, 76
LORSCH, J. W., 122, 141
Lower East Side, description of, 13

M

MALLUCCIO, A. N., 67, 141
Managerial function, 97
Managers, 11
MARLOW, W. D., 67, 141
MAYER, J., 20, 141
Means and ends, 37–54
Meetings: between conflicting organizations, 105; with workers from other agencies, 67–69
MELD, M., 10, 22, 141
Mental health services, 104–106, 112, 113
MIDDLEMAN, R., 103, 104, 141
MODE, F., 70, 73
Model Cities Program, 5
Money management, 122
Monitoring: issues involving, 111–117; opposition to, 57; by SWAs, 69, 70
Monroe House, 32, 70, 106
Multiproblem families, 5
Multiservice centers, 5

N

Name, LESFU, change of, 28
Negotiations with providers, client's inability in, 123

Neighborhood service centers, 5
Network therapy, 35, 36

O

Operationalization of program, 37–38, 120
Outcome measures, 9, 10
Outreach programs: development of, 24; local workers and, 56, 57; methods of, 97, 98; training and, 64, 65; and volunteers, 46

P

Paying for needed services, 123
PENN, W.: and client independence, 110; and confidentiality, 113; and family service contracts, 102, 103
Performance of agency, 95–120
PERROW, C., 141
Personalities of workers, 116
PFEFFER, J., 122, 141
Placement, average term of, 117
Policy formulation, xi, 23–36
Poverty program of 1960s, 28–36, 128
PRESSMAN, J., xi, 125, 141
Prevention priorities, 26, 27, 48
Problem definition, 13–19
Problem recognition, 123
Procedures and design problems, 129
Process studies, 9
Program design, 28–34, 121–137
Program evaluators, 11
Program instigators, 12–22
Programmatic options, 10
Provider issues, 124
Public agencies and private agencies, 5, 132, 133
Public assistance problems, 122

R

RACHAL, P., 133, 142
Rationality, 30
Recognition of problems, 123
REDBURN, S., 134, 141
REID, W., 126, 141

Religion, 32

Remediation programs, 29

Reorganization of government, 7

Research, xi; board's concern over, 74; limitations on, 57; and service, 47–53; use of, 130

Resource file of neighborhood residents, 87

Resources and design problems, 129

REUVENI, V., 142

RHODES, S. L., 110, 117, 131, 141

RICHARDSON, E., 6

RITTEL, H., 78, 141

Role-playing exercises, 83, 103, 104

ROSENBERG, M. L., 131, 135, 141

RUE, H., xii; background of, 13–19; communcating with, 94; and funding, 25–28; and index of high-risk families, 49; and program design, 28–31; and staff problems, 52, 73, 76, 77; style of, 24

S

SAHLEIN, W. J., 5, 141

SALANCIK, G. R., 122, 141

SAVANT, S.: and goal attainment scale, 47; hiring of, 38–41; and social historian's task, 50-52

SCHUMAN, K., 11, 142

SEBRING, R. H., 142

Self-design model, 122

Self-help programs, 87

SELZNICK, P., 37, 142

Service integration models, 7, 10, 134, 135

Service organization, 28

Sex of client, 108, 109

Shared tensions, 92, 93. *See also* Tension

Signatures of clients, 108

Social history, xii, 50, 51

Social reform, 136

Social settlements, 4

Social work associates (SWAs): and case status reports, 85; convening meetings and, 67; and evaluation, fears of, 66; expectations of, 86, 87; firing of, 42; hiring of, 40, 56;

job requirements for, 81; role behavior of, 103, 104; as role models, 98

SOFPAINT, H., 114

Spanish teams, 9, 32

SPECHT, H., 9, 10, 23, 35, 135, 140

Special Services for Children (SSC): city team from, 113; comparison of LESFU and, 132; cooperation with, 107, 108; reports to, 104; legal aid versus, 105; referrals from, 30

Specialists, 11, 135

SPECK, R. V., 36, 46, 142

SSC. *See* Special Services for Children

Staff, 38–41; and design problems, 128. *See also* Training

STEIN, T. J., 130, 142

Stress and strain on workers, 8, 81, 82, 107

Structural service delivery, 103

Supervision of workers, 61–64

SWAs. *See* Social work associates

T

Tables: agencies providing services, 118; social work associate case status report, 85; sources of high-risk cases, 96; unshared tensions, 93

Taking action, refusal in, 123

TASTE, S., xiii, 107

Teams, 9; board and team leaders, 70–78; and community residents, 40; integration of, 60, 61; and local residents, 56–60; makeup of, 32; and monitoring, 111–117; theory of, 34

Tension, mechanisms for reduction of, 83, 84, 91–94

Term of placement, 117

Theory of design, 121–124

TIMMS, N., 20, 141

Training, 64–67; in-service programs, 33; need for, 83, 84; social historian present at, 51, 52; weekly training sessions, 61

Transportation problems of clients, 123

U

Unemployment, 13, 122

V

Value conflicts, 10, 11
Voluntary organization, 28, 29
Volunteer workers, 45, 46

W

WEBBER, M., 1, 78, 141
Weekly training sessions, 61
WEICK, K. E., 122, 142
WEISSMAN, H. H., xiii, xvii, xviii, 32, 34, 142
White House Conference on Children (1909), 3
WILDAVSKY, A., xi, 125, 141
WILLS, C., 99
WILSON, J. Q., 133, 142
WINDWARD, T., xiix, 111, 114
Work agreement, 100, 101